REAL SCOTLAND
THE INSIDER'S GUIDE

Published 2010 | Text © VisitScotland 2010 | Photography © Scottish Viewpoint, VisitScotland and Paul Tomkins
Design by Blue-Chip Marketing | All rights reserved | This guide is printed on recycled content paper

EUROPE & SCOTLAND
European Regional Development Fund
Investing in your Future

Front Cover - VIEW TO THE BLACK CUILLIN RIDGE, ISLE OF SKYE

REAL SCOTLAND
THE INSIDER'S GUIDE

SHETLAND ISLES

FOULA

LERWICK

KEY TO MAP

⊕ INTERNATIONAL AIRPORT
⊕ REGIONAL AIRPORT
⫻ MOTORWAYS
╱ ROADS
RAILWAYS
CAR FERRY ROUTES
PASSENGER FERRY ROUTES

FAIR ISLE

ORKNEY ISLES

KIRKWALL

OUTER HEBRIDES

DURNESS   THURSO

WICK

STORNOWAY

ULLAPOOL

FRASERBURGH

DINGWALL   ELGIN

PORTREE   INVERNESS

BENBECULA   **ISLE OF SKYE**   KYLE OF LOCHALSH

ABERDEEN

BARRA

CAIRNGORMS NATIONAL PARK

MALLAIG   FORT WILLIAM

TIREE

OBAN   *LOCH LOMOND & THE TROSSACHS NATIONAL PARK*   PERTH   **DUNDEE**

INNER HEBRIDES   KIRKCALDY

STIRLING   **EDINBURGH**

GREENOCK   **GLASGOW**

ISLAY   KILMARNOCK   GALASHIELS

AYR   PRESTWICK

CAMPBELTOWN

ISLANDS OF THE CLYDE ESTUARY   DUMFRIES

STRANRAER

CONTENTS

INTRODUCTION

Why do the locals never frequent the places where the tourists flock? What do they know that visitors don't? The world over this phenomenon holds true. Down cobbled backstreets and leafy byways, along unmarked paths and beyond echoing courtyards, the locals guard their best-kept secrets: little gems of pubs and restaurants, deserted white beaches and dancing waterfalls, ancient ruins and silent haunts that time has forgotten.

And Scotland is no exception to this rule: beneath its eye-catching facade lie hidden depths, an amazing array of authentic experiences just waiting to be discovered. To help you along, we've lifted the lid on the 'Real Scotland' - with this exclusive guide drawn from the nation's collective consciousness. We started with a focus on the islands to uncover as many hidden gems as possible and then rounded off our tour on the Scottish mainland.

How did we do it? Simple - we asked the locals!

1.

2.

3.

1. TRAIGH AN IAR,
   HORGABOST,
   ISLE OF HARRIS

2. LOCH TROOL,
   DUMFRIES & GALLOWAY

3. VIEW OF LOCH LOMOND

4. ST CUTHBERT'S PARISH CHURCH BELOW EDINBURGH CASTLE, EDINBURGH

5. STANDING STONES OF CALANAIS, ISLE OF LEWIS

1.

2.

1. BRODICK BAY TOWARDS
   GOAT FELL, ISLE OF ARRAN

2. MOUNT STUART,
   ISLE OF BUTE

3. LOCHRANZA CASTLE,
   ISLE OF ARRAN

4. WAVERLEY PADDLE
   STEAMER, ISLE OF ARRAN

ISLANDS OF THE CLYDE ESTUARY

It was the Scottish engineer Henry Bell who saw the potential of the sea channels around the fascinating islands of the Clyde and the burgeoning city of Glasgow, and successfully pioneered the steamboat allowing them to be explored.

Bell's 'Comet', the first passenger steamboat service in Europe, sailed in 1812 and soon numerous Clyde-built steamers were carrying delighted city folk 'doon the watter' for a relaxing break on the lush islands of Arran and Bute.

The era of the Clyde steamers is long gone, though the last seagoing paddle steamer in the world, the famous Waverley, will

4.

still transport you in style to the idyllic islands of the Clyde during the summer months. Even aboard a regular ferry, approaching Arran, Bute or Great Cumbrae is an exhilarating experience.

Arran, with its mountainous north and low lying south, is known as Scotland in miniature and is one of the country's most beautiful islands.

3.

Bute boasts the charming town of Rothesay with its classic Victorian seaside facade and Great Cumbrae has lovely Millport with its tiny yet remarkable Cathedral of the Isles.

Arran, Bute and Great Cumbrae are all perfect island escapes, yet are so close to vibrant Glasgow. Enjoy the thrill of a brief sea voyage and linger a while on these islands.

enthusiast with climbing, golfing, and fishing, while the island is famed for its excellent produce, including cheese, oysters, and oatcakes.

In the heart of Rothesay, Bute's main town, is Rothesay Castle, a remarkable survivor from the 13th century, built to an unusual circular design and features an impressive moat. The castle fell under attack on many occasions by the Vikings and was once captured by the English before being retaken by Robert the Bruce. A few miles from Rothesay is the lovely village of Port Bannatyne, facing out to the picturesque Kames Bay.

5.

7.

6.

Brodick Castle and Country Park on Arran is, in fact, the only island country park in Britain. The castle offers 600 years of history and fascinating artefacts while the highlight of the lovely gardens is the rhododendron collection. Arran also has much for the sports

FACT

The Highland Boundary Fault cuts through Arran, explaining the sharp contrast between the jagged peaks of the north and rolling farmland of the south, and that Scotland in miniature tag. Nowhere else in the country has such geological complexities within such a small area.

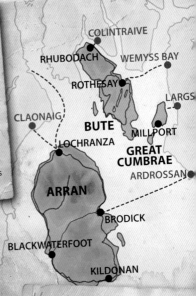

Hidden Gem

Ascog Fernery, Isle of Bute.

Ascog Hall Fernery, on Bute, is most definitely a labour of love. It is the authentic restoration of a sunken Victorian fernery that was accidentally discovered in the 1980s in ruinous condition by the new owners of Ascog Hall. Miraculously, one large fern survived and a huge specimen of Todea Barbara is there today. The fern is said to be 1,000 years old or more.

Tell your friends when you get back

Mount Stuart, on Bute, is an exuberant Victorian mansion, home to the Stuarts of Bute, descendants of the Royal House of Stuart. The flamboyant house and extravagant gardens reflect the artistic, religious, and astrological passions of the 3rd Marquess of Bute. Why not take a behind the scenes tour and discover the world's first domestic heated indoor swimming pool?

How to get there

Arran: The ferry from Ardrossan to Brodick takes just under an hour with frequent daily services. There is also the ferry to Lochranza from Claonaig on the Kintyre Peninsula.

Bute: The ferry from Wemyss Bay to Rothesay takes just over 30 minutes with frequent daily services. There is also a short crossing from Colintraive on the Cowal Peninsula to Rhubodach at the north end of Bute.

Great Cumbrae: The ferry from Largs takes only 10 minutes with frequent daily crossings.

5. MILLPORT CATHEDRAL, GREAT CUMBRAE
6. BRODICK CASTLE, ISLE OF ARRAN
7. ROTHESAY CASTLE, ISLE OF BUTE

THE INNER HEBRIDES

As the ferry casts off to the isolated Inner Hebrides, you will feel a certain sense of adventure.

Consider these islands as a menu where you can sample flavours that include Islay's peaty whiskies and the oysters farmed on Colonsay. Romantic, rugged, and wild in varying degrees, there is something magical about these peaceful gems.

The Gulf Stream takes the edge off winter's frost, nurturing the gardens on Gigha and Colonsay, while the name Lismore comes from the Gaelic for 'great garden'. Low-lying Tiree is one of the sunniest isles in the UK with low rainfall statistics and high winds - another meteorological quirk.

1.

1. SCARINISH HARBOUR, ISLE OF TIREE
2. THE PAPS OF JURA, FROM ISLAY, INNER HEBRIDES
3. SUNSET OVER THE ISLANDS OF RUM AND EIGG
4. CALGARY BAY, ISLE OF MULL

Enjoy Mull's breathtaking seascapes and soaring sea eagles, spot otters on Jura, or head to the Small Isles to really get away from it all. Rum boasts a population of manx shearwaters which dig nesting burrows in the ground.

Coll and Tiree lie close together and can be accessed via the same ferry link. Tiree is famed for its fertile sandy soil and is sometimes called the 'garden of the Hebrides'. It's a favourite with surfers, thanks to the open beaches and the sheer size of the waves here.

5.

6.

Farming, distilling, fishing and crafting are widespread and there are good accommodation and eating options. But, when the Atlantic breakers roll in on some empty, dazzling Hebridean beach, you will feel that, at least in part, wild nature still rules.

Modern ferries connect all of the Inner Hebridean islands with the mainland, yet there is still a degree of remoteness about the landscapes here. Colonsay is a favourite with many, a real treasure and one of the most secluded isles. A superb variety of habitats await, from tidal sandflats, hidden coves, beaches and cliffs to moorland, lochs and unusual dwarf woodland. Birdwatchers come to see the rare chough, taking time to look out for this distinctive red-legged crow.

Islay and Jura are a contrasting pair. There is nothing quite like the taste of west coast whisky and nowhere is this more apparent than the Isle of Islay. Travel by plane or ferry for tastings at any of the eight malt distilleries, where the 'uisge beatha' (water of life) truly represents the peaty landscapes, rich farmland and beautiful bays of this tranquil place.

By contrast, Jura is one of the last wildernesses in Scotland. An encounter with deer is inevitable here and strolling around the island provides a feeling of splendid isolation.

Most visitors take the car as far as the road permits and many

Mull is a larger island and it is well worth touring, particularly along the dramatic west coastline. Depart on a boat trip to Staffa and capture the magic of Fingal's Cave, then see if you can catch a glimpse of puffins. Tobermory's colourful seafront attracts lots of visitors and

7.

continue on foot to pass Barnhill, where the writer George Orwell wrote his futuristic novel '1984'. At the north end of Jura, visit the Corryvreckan Whirlpool which is the third largest in the world.

8.

5. BALNAHARD BAY, ISLE OF COLONSAY

6. ARDBEG DISTILLERY, ISLAY

7. THE ONLY ROAD ON THE ISLE OF JURA

8. A PUFFIN, OFF THE ISLE OF MULL

The unspoilt environment of the west coast nurtures top quality farmed shellfish. Island Mussel Stew is a classic dish. As well as mussels, other shellfish, including oysters or cockles, can be substituted.

Island Mussel Stew Recipe

COOKING METHOD

After scrubbing mussels, discarding any open, place in a pan with wine, cover and bring to boil. Simmer gently for 3 minutes until all mussels open. Strain liquid and keep aside. Remove mussels from shell, discarding beards. Melt butter, stir in flour, add mussel liquid, continuing to stir, then add warmed milk. Add finely chopped onion and simmer until cooked. Add seasoning, parsley then mussels and cream. Do not allow to boil, or mussels may go rubbery. Serve in soup plates.

INGREDIENTS

30 Mussels
Tbsp Butter
Tbsp Flour
1 Onion
1 Cup Milk
White wine
Salt, pepper
Parsley
Cream

was recently used in the children's television series Balamory. Many also make the trip to Iona, a spiritual haven where St Columba spread the word of Christianity.

Tell your friends when you get back

Formed from basaltic columns, the eerie echoes of Fingal's Cave, reached from Jura, inspired the great composer Mendelssohn to write the beautiful 'Hebrides Overture' that evokes the rolling waves and solitude found here. Wordsworth, Keats and Lord Tennyson all spent time on the Isle of Staffa and J.M.W. Turner painted 'Staffa, Fingal's Cave' in 1832.

The Small Isles of Muck, Eigg, Canna and Rum are varied. Muck boasts fertile farmland, Eigg holds a strong sense of community, Canna has high basaltic cliffs, while Rum offers formidable volcanic peaks and a distinctive castle.

Gigha lies in the shelter of the long arm of Kintyre and is known for its mild climate. Proof of this are the gardens of Achamore House, one of the few places where camellias grow in thickets.

FACT

Islay is reckoned to have the finest surviving Celtic carved cross, the extraordinary Kildalton Cross. This 8th century ringed cross was carved from a single piece of epidiorite rock. Find it near the end of the road running east from Port Ellen, after 7 miles, well beyond the Laphroaig and Ardbeg Distilleries. Continue just a little further for the sheltered east facing Claggan Bay.

Food Tip

The award-winning Tobermory fish and chip van on Mull serves the best of seafood, landed fresh from the surrounding waters, that is cooked to order. The setting on the waterfront is just fantastic.

9. TOBERMORY, ISLE OF MULL

10. ACHAMORE GARDENS, ISLE OF GIGHA

11. FINGAL'S CAVE, ISLE OF STAFFA

How to get there

Islay: Fly direct from Glasgow in 40 minutes.

Colonsay: Ferry service from Oban with an additional service from Kennacraig during the summer months.

Coll and Tiree: Ferry links from Oban. Some sailings go on to the island of Barra.

Islay and Jura: Ferry links from Kennacraig to Port Ellen and Port Askaig. Feolin on Jura is a short crossing from Port Askaig. Kennacraig to Port Ellen is 2 hours 20 minutes.

Mull and Iona: Oban to Craignure (Mull) takes around 45 minutes. Note other link, Lochaline to Fishnish (Mull) takes 15 minutes. Mull (Fionnphort) to Iona has frequent daily ferry services taking 10 minutes.

Small Isles: Regular pattern of ferry services (except Sundays) to various islands from Mallaig.

Gigha: Daily ferries, taking 20 minutes from Tayinloan.

CANNA

MALLAIG

RUM

TO SOUTH UIST

EIGG

MUCK

TO BARRA

KILCHOAN   LAGA

COLL

TOBERMORY   LOCHALINE   LISMORE

TIREE

MULL   FISHNISH
CRAIGNURE

OBAN

IONA

FIONNPHORT

COLONSAY   JURA

ISLAY
PORT ASKAIG   FEOLIN

TO
KENNACRAIG

BOWMORE

GIGHA
TAYINLOAN

PORT
ELLEN

1. ELGOL, ISLE OF SKYE

2. HORSE RIDING BY A LOCH,
   ISLE OF SKYE

3. WATERSTEIN HEAD
   AND MOONEN BAY, ISLE OF SKYE

4. ROAD BRIDGE TO SKYE,
   AT KYLE OF LOCHALSH

5. SUNSET OVER THE CUILLIN HILLS,
   ISLE OF SKYE

THE ISLE OF SKYE

The Gaelic poetic name for the island, 'Eilean a' Cheó', means island of the cloud or mist. Yes, it rains sometimes, but when the clouds lift, the landscapes are so breathtaking you can forgive everything.

'Over the sea to Skye' (along with the 'The Bonnie Banks o' Loch Lomond') must be one of the best known songs of Scotland. Naturally, the Skye Bridge makes for the simplest route over the sea from the mainland, while the Mallaig to Armadale ferry allows a pleasing loop on or off the island if you are touring. The third and historic mainland connection is the Glenelg to Kylerhea service, at an ancient crossing place on the Kyle of Lochalsh narrows.

5.

It's Glen Brittle and Elgol for picture postcard views, fine dining, adventure sports, cruises and excursions, castle visiting or just pottering along enjoying the scenery. If you're new to the Cuillins, then hire a guide or join a guided walk. The English mountain writer W. A. Poucher in his classic guide 'The Scottish Peaks' remarks that the summits of the Cuillins "usually involve more rock climbing, and other than Bruach na Frithe, are not for the ordinary pedestrian". Luckily, 'ordinary pedestrians' have plenty of other places to walk on this wonderful island.

4.

6.

The pinnacle called the Old Man of Storr is obvious from the road. A little further, the Quiraing above Staffin Bay is even more peculiar. Geologists describe this area as a good example of 'rotational slippage' - basically, over millions of years, the cliff edges are slowly breaking off in great rocky chunks and falling over.

Though the Cuillin hills are the most famous of Skye's landforms, ancient volcanoes created much of the rest of Skye's spectacular landscapes. This is very noticeable travelling north from the main town of Portree. The Trotternish Ridge, the cliff-like edge of a lava sheet, runs for about 20 miles.

7.

Real People Tips

Gary Sutherland, Scottish guidebook author, is a regular visitor to Skye and the island is one of his favourite destinations. He points out you can find one of the world's top restaurants on Skye. "The Three Chimneys, near Dunvegan, is famed for the quality of its cuisine, the wonderful seafood and game, and the restaurant's signature dish, hot marmalade pudding." Not far from The Three Chimneys is Talisker Distillery, the only malt whisky distillery on Skye. Take the tour and enjoy sampling one of Scotland's finest whiskies.

Hints & Tips

If touring northwards on Skye, having come off the Armadale ferry, it's well worth diverting round the Tarskavaig loop. Look for it signed left for Achnacloich, Tarskavaig and Tokavaig at Sabhal Mór Ostaig - the Gaelic college. Soon, superb views open up over the peninsula of Strathaird and the spiky mountain Blaven, to the Cuillins beyond. On the approach to Tokavaig, park carefully by the shore and you can walk round to the ruined Dunscaith Castle on its headland. Once a Clan Donald stronghold it was abandoned in the early 17th century - hence not a lot left but a great setting.

FACT

Skye was the last place in Scotland that still had sea eagles, up until 1916, when they were persecuted to extinction. A reintroduction programme was started on Rum, and they first bred on Skye by 1987. Now 20% of Scotland's sea eagle population breed here. Look for them from headlands near Portree.

Tell your friends when you get back

The Glenelg Ferry Service is community owned and really needs your support. It's a short 5 minute crossing, summer only. Watch out for the resident sea eagle on the way and also the skipper's dog, who helps with the mooring ropes.

8.

6. THE TROTTERNISH RIDGE, ISLE OF SKYE

7. THE OLD MAN OF STORR, ISLE OF SKYE

8. DUNVEGAN CASTLE, ISLE OF SKYE

Myths & Legends

The Fairy Flag of Dunvegan is one of the most unusual artefacts to be seen in Dunvegan Castle, seat of the chief of the Clan MacLeod. An ancient piece of silk, many legends are associated with it. It is said to have been acquired by a chief who married a local fairy (Gaelic bean-shith, hence banshee). It has, of course, magic powers and has twice saved the clan, in times of war and pestilence. However, it can only be used three times, after that, the fairies have to take it back. Many MacLeods believe in its powers. Apparently, in World War II, airmen named MacLeod often carried a picture of it in their wallets, as a talisman to guarantee their safe return.

THE OUTER HEBRIDES

The Outer Hebrides, or Western Isles, is an idyllic archipelago off the west coast of Scotland with the open Atlantic beyond and is famed for its dazzling white sandy beaches. A greater proportion of the population speak Gaelic here than anywhere else in Scotland, though the islanders are bilingual.

In this remote paradise you can fish, golf, walk, go birdwatching or pony trekking, track down some fine craftwork, enjoy the local museums and get a proper sense of the heritage of these islands. But there is something about the experience of just being here that makes the Outer Hebrides distinct from any other part of Scotland. It has to do with the more gentle pace of life, the strong sense of the past and the manner in which the houses seem to cling to the wide open loch-dotted landscape - something you'll notice especially in the Uists. It's just that little bit different, and definitely romantic.

Which is why, in spite of there being plenty to do, you may find yourself sitting watching the waves and simply unwinding - unless you happen to be a keen birdwatcher or wildlife photographer, in which case

1.

2.

1. LOCHMADDY, NORTH UIST

2. TRAIGH IAR BEACH,
    NORTH UIST

3. THE BUTT OF LEWIS,
    ISLE OF LEWIS

4. RUINS OF DUN CARLOWAY
    BROCH, ISLE OF LEWIS

5. TRAIGH AN IAR, HORGABOST,
    ISLE OF HARRIS

you'll spend much of your time gasping at the sight of raptors like short-eared owls and harriers, or scarce northern species, especially divers, common enough to go almost unremarked. You may even get blasé about spotting otters.

These islands form an arc of about 130 miles, so remember to allow enough time. Consider taking the ferry from Ullapool in the Highlands to Stornoway on Lewis and tour the islands from north to south, leaving from Castlebay on Barra for a return to the mainland at Oban. Many of the islands are linked by causeway and those that are not have great ferry links. Part of the joy is in journeying around the Outer Hebrides and noting the definite contrasts between the islands.

The Outer Hebrides is one of the most sparsely populated parts of Scotland, with an overall population of around 26,000 and many of the islands are uninhabited.

The character of each island is different. Lewis has by far the largest town, Stornoway, while the hinterland is characterised by miles of rolling moor, with the settlements mainly on the coast. The Blackhouse at Arnol, a preserved traditional home, is the best place to get an insight into the former way of life. The famous Standing Stones of Calanais are the high profile attraction, sometimes called 'Scotland's Stonehenge'.

7.

8.

6.

Harris is more mountainous than Lewis and boasts some spectacular beaches on its west coast. Plus there are still places, the Luskentyre Harris Tweed Company for instance, where you can see the famous luxury cloth being woven.

The Uists and Benbecula offer a fascinating mix of landscapes with beaches and machair to the west, moors studded with lochs - there are said to be 6,000 lochs in the Outer Hebrides - and rugged hills to the east. These islands are a haven for birdwatchers.

10.

9.

Eriskay is a tiny gem of an island surrounded by sparkling blue sea and has an association with Bonnie Prince Charlie in that he landed from France on a beach, now known as Prince's Beach, at the south end of Eriskay.

6. BEACH NEAR LOSGAINTIR, ISLE OF HARRIS
7. ARNOL BLACKHOUSE MUSEUM, ISLE OF LEWIS
8. STANDING STONES OF CALANAIS, ISLE OF LEWIS
9. BEACH AT TOLSTA, ISLE OF LEWIS
10. LOCHMADDY, NORTH UIST

Hidden Gem

Loch Druidibeg National Nature Reserve, South Uist.

Loch Druidibeg National Nature Reserve on South Uist stretches from the Atlantic coast to almost the other side of the island. The reserve features a stunning variety of habitats and is very wild and picturesque. There is a good chance of spotting otters and the western part of the reserve is the place to listen for the elusive corncrake, a rarely sighted bird noted for its distinctive scratchy call.

Real People Tips

Local historian Bill Lawson, from Northton on Harris, has an encyclopaedic knowledge of the area. He has a quick tip for a rewarding excursion. "An easy walk is over Northton Machair to the ruined Teampall. Flowers, wildlife, history and the ruins of a pre-Reformation church. What more could you ask for?"

Barra is another island of great character and interest, its main town Castlebay guarded by the stunning Kisimul Castle in the bay. Beyond Barra lie the islands of Vatersay and Mingulay with the possibility of a boat trip to see the huge sea cliffs.

11.

12.

11. KISIMUL CASTLE, CASTLEBAY, ISLE OF BARRA

12. VATERSAY BAY, ISLE OF VATERSAY OFF BARRA

Local Dialect

As the Outer Hebrides is the heartland of the Gaelic language, here is a short glossary of Gaelic to help you on your visit.

Gaelic	English
Madainn mhath (pronounced Mateen Vah)	Good morning
Feasgar math (Fesker Mah)	Good afternoon/ Good evening
Oidhche mhath (Oy-ke Vah)	Good night
Is mise (Is Meesha)	My name is
Ciamar a tha thu? (Ci-mar a ha oo?)	How are you?
Co as a tha thu? (Co as a ha oo?)	Where are you from?
Tha mi a (Ha mi a)	I am from
Tha mi gu math (Ha me goo mah)	I am well
Tapadh leat (Tap-ah lat)	Thank you

Hidden Gem

Beinn Sciathan (Ben Scrien), Eriskay.

Climb to the highest point on Eriskay, Beinn Sciathan (Ben Scrien), and you'll probably meet the local Eriskay ponies on the way. It isn't a difficult walk and you will be rewarded with great views south towards Barra, and north across the Sound of Eriskay to the Uists. The plaintive whistle in the background will probably be a golden plover, adding to the atmosphere.

Tell your friends when you get back

It was still highly unusual back in 1949 for a film to be made almost entirely on location. Nevertheless, when Ealing Studios decided to make Whisky Galore, based on Compton Mackenzie's comic novel, they filmed almost all the scenes on the Isle of Barra. The real life SS Politician with its cargo of whisky was in fact wrecked off neighbouring Eriskay. The only pub on Eriskay, 'Am Politician' actually has a couple of bottles of the salvaged whisky on display.

Myths & Legends

There are many stories about the Blue Men of the Minch, the spirits said to haunt the channel between the Outer Hebrides and mainland Scotland. Some say they are storm kelpies who demand respect. Others think they are fallen angels who landed in the sea. A local minister in Victorian times swore that one had followed his boat. If you happen to be out on the Minch and a Blue Man approaches, it is important to know some Gaelic, as that is how these spirits converse. You may be questioned and required to answer in rhyming couplets.

How to get there

Fly: There are flight connections from the Scottish mainland to airports at Stornoway, Benbecula and Barra. The latter is unique in that it is the only airport in the world with scheduled flights landing on a beach.

Ferry: Mainland ferry ports with links to the Outer Hebrides are: Ullapool for Stornoway; Uig on Skye for Tarbert (Harris) and Lochmaddy (North Uist); Oban for Lochboisdale (South Uist) and Barra. The main inter-island ferries are Leverburgh (Harris) to Berneray (for North Uist) and also Eriskay to Barra.

PORT OF NESS
ARNOL
STORNOWAY
CALLANISH
LEWIS
TO ULLAPOOL
TARBERT
HARRIS
LEVERBURGH
BERNERAY
OTTERNISH
NORTH UIST
UIG
LOCHMADDY
BENBECULA
SOUTH UIST
LOCHBOISDALE
ISLE OF ERISKAY
BARRA
TO OBAN
CASTLEBAY
TO OBAN

1. WEST COAST OF MAINLAND,
    YESNABY, ORKNEY

2. WAREBETH BEACH AND ISLE OF HOY,
    NEAR STROMNESS, ORKNEY

3. THE RING OF BRODGAR, ORKNEY

4. THE OLD MAN OF HOY, ORKNEY

5. WATERFRONT AT STROMNESS, ORKNEY

THE ORKNEY ISLES

If you stand on the beach at Thurso, or on the breezy cliff top by Dunnet Head, you'll see Orkney quite plainly, filling the horizon with the sight of its sandstone, layered cliffs which give nothing away, not even a hint of the wonder that lies beyond.

4.

swings sharply into Hoy Sound is the truth about Orkney revealed - it's a friendly, green place where a quarter of the workforce is in agriculture.

5.

Take to the water, across the swells of the Pentland Firth, and the sense of mystery deepens. Travellers line the rail of the boat to watch the spectacular stack of the Old Man of Hoy slide past on the starboard side, though even this landmark is dwarfed by the view of the cliffs of St John's Head that lie beyond.

Up to this point, it's all soaring verticals and seabirds along the red rock of Hoy. Not until the ferry

Orkney is a place that makes a big first impression, from Stromness looking like a Scandinavian settlement, to the huge St Magnus Cathedral in Kirkwall, which dominates the skyline as a reminder that this little community was, in its day, an important religious centre in the Viking seas. Even the quality of the finely designed jewellery in the Kirkwall craft shops hints that this is a place of substance and trade, the cruise ship clientele echoing the merchants and traders that have stopped off here for centuries.

Friendly and with a continuity of settlement and heritage second to none, Orkney is so rewarding. The soft accent of the friendly islanders is just the most pleasing cadence you'll ever hear.

Orkney simply offers a different perspective on a holiday in the UK, not just because of its wealth of prehistory, but because of the strong ties to the history and heritage which are still there for all to see and hear. After all, the rhythms of the pleasing accents heard today still echo the old language, Norn (descended from Old Norse) that died out to be replaced by the lowland Scots and English tongue. In short, this is all to do with Scandinavia, with no connections to Gaeldom.

In the old red sandstone with its convenient horizontal beds, the early settlers found good building stone. Visit Skara Brae, perhaps the most extraordinary archaeological site in Britain, and afterwards you'll catch yourself eyeing up lintel shapes and blocks lying on the adjacent beach and be itching to build your own Stone Age shelter.

6.

There are still discoveries being made today - the so-called 'Orkney Venus' was dug out of the dunes on the island of Westray in 2009, and was the earliest representation of the human figure ever found in Scotland.

7.

In more recent historic terms, St Magnus Cathedral and the Earl's Palace opposite should be visited when in Kirkwall. The ruined palace is sometimes described as the finest example of French Renaissance architecture in Scotland. Also on the 'must see' list is the Stromness Museum, where you can uncover the background of the scuttling German battle-fleet in Scapa Flow at the end of World War I. Along with the fascinating collection at Lyness on Hoy that portrays the role of this once-vital naval anchorage, it is a reminder that Orkney's story is a complex one. The common element is. its importance, culturally and historically, in these northern waters.

6. SKARA BRAE, ORKNEY
7. ST MAGNUS CATHEDRAL, KIRKWALL, ORKNEY

Tell your friends when you get back

Scapa Flow is a magnificent natural anchorage, so it's no surprise it was so important for the Royal Navy in times of war. The Scapa Flow Visitor Centre at Lyness, Hoy, is a great place to visit. Some historians also think that the air conflict of the Battle of Britain actually started over Orkney. Radar was first used to direct British aircraft defending Scapa Flow against enemy raids, a 'dress rehearsal' three months before the more famous battles in the English Channel.

Food Tip

The Watersound Restaurant in the Sands Hotel at Burray Village embraces its location in a former herring station with a nautical-themed decor. Visitors and locals fill the restaurant regularly for a chance to enjoy the à la carte menu that uses as much local produce as possible. Specialities include the scallops and the squid or you can try the catch of the day.

How to get there

Fly: Kirkwall has air links from Glasgow, Edinburgh, Aberdeen and Inverness. There are internal flights to Westray, Papa Westray, North Ronaldsay, Sanday, Stronsay and Eday. This includes the famous 'world's shortest scheduled flight' - under 2 minutes between Westray and Papa Westray. You even get a certificate to prove it!

Ferry: Ferries link Scrabster to Stromness, Aberdeen to Kirkwall and Gills Bay to St Margaret's Hope and during summer you can catch the ferry between John o'Groats and Burwick. There is a good network of inter-island ferries, connecting mainland Orkney to the thirteen islands.

NORTH RONALDSAY
PAPA WESTRAY
WESTRAY
SANDAY
ROUSAY
STRONSAY
EDAY
TO LERWICK
STROMNESS
KIRKWALL
TO ABERDEEN
ST MARGARET'S HOPE
SOUTH RONALDSAY
HOY
BURWICK
GILLS BAY
JOHN O'GROATS
SCRABSTER

THE SHETLAND ISLES

This is another Scotland entirely. It has nothing to do with tartan and soaring mountains, instead discover an incredible 1,000-plus km of coastline, an abundance of rare wildlife and a Viking heritage second to none.

1.

accommodating more than a million nesting seabirds - look out for puffins as they waddle along grassy cliffs, and the razorbills and guillemots which sit in their thousands like black-and-white bottles stacked on narrow shelves along huge cliff-faces. These great bird-cities can be reached on foot or by boat (or simply join one of the many excellent tour operators).

In short, Shetland is an adventure - a not to be missed experience of a truly cosmopolitan place, not on the edge, but in the centre of the northern seas.

It is often said that no part of Shetland is more than 5 miles from the sea. Inevitably, then, it forms a backdrop and constant theme. Its archaeology and ancient places, like Jarlshof, Old Scatness or the magnificent Broch of Mousa are close by the sea. Shetland has five main seabird colonies

2.

1. JARLSHOF SETTLEMENT, SHETLAND
2. MOUSA BROCH ON THE ISLAND OF MOUSA, SHETLAND
3. ISLAND OF UNST, SHETLAND
4. SANDS OF BRECKON, ISLAND OF YELL, SHETLAND
5. THE GAADA STACK, THE ISLAND OF FOULA, SHETLAND

Naturally, the magnificent coastal scenery, the likes of which includes Sumburgh or Eshaness, are all on the list of marine 'must sees'.

6.

When it comes to history, the arrival of the Vikings marked a vital turning point for Shetland, with reminders of these ferocious warriors everywhere, from place names such as St Olaf Street to relics, which continue to be unearthed across the isles. In fact, Britain's most northerly inhabited island, Unst, has the highest number of rural Viking longhouses in the world. Witness this legacy at Europe's largest annual fire festival Up Helly Aa. This spectacular event is held in January, where you can watch the Viking Jarl Squad parade through Lerwick with burning torches before setting alight the replica longship. There are local celebrations throughout February and March, all of which culminate in singing and dancing long into the night.

And perhaps it is the long winter nights that means Shetland folk are always ready to celebrate and enjoy music. The traditional music of Shetland certainly revolves around the fiddle. It was easy to transport and as Shetland folk have always been traders and

7.

fishermen, historically, they picked up influences from other parts of the world. Out of this melodic mix there evolved a Shetland sound. It had links to the Hardanger fiddle across the North Sea, certainly, and had mainland Scotland and some Irish elements too but it formed the core of a thriving music scene that continues today. You will find musical events galore on these islands, all year round. A well timed visit to The Lounge Bar in Lerwick will more than likely reward visitors with an informal fiddle session.

6.   CLIFFS OF ESHANESS, SHETLAND

7.   TRADITIONAL SCOTTISH FOLK MUSIC, LERWICK, SHETLAND

Tell your friends when you get back

You can join the wardens on the early morning round at the Fair Isle Lodge and Bird Observatory for a chance to see rare migrant birds. At only 3 miles long and lying halfway between Shetland and Orkney, Fair Isle is famous for its knitwear, but the island has long been a favourite spot for birdwatchers. For some 60 years, this landmark observatory has played a pioneering role in the study of bird migration. The observatory lodge offers comfortable accommodation and guests are invited to join staff for the bird log at 9.30pm before retiring to the bar for a nightcap.

How to get there

Fly: Shetland has daily flights from Edinburgh, Glasgow, Aberdeen, Inverness and Orkney. Shetland's main airport is at Sumburgh, 25 miles south of Lerwick. Car hire is available there and the airport has taxis and a bus connection with Lerwick.

Ferry: Sail to Shetland (Lerwick), daily all year round on comfortable cruising vessels. Travel time from Aberdeen is 12-13 hours. It is an overnight crossing and a great experience - look out for whales, dolphins and seabirds!

Real People Tips

Alexis Odie is the manager of the Shetland Soap Company in Lerwick and looks after the UK's most northerly skin care company. She gets ideas from the natural environment of Shetland, its sea and weather. "This is one of my special places: I love to visit the Old Haa in Burravoe, Yell where you get a glimpse of bygone times in the museum, but my favourite part is having a nice coffee and some of their lovingly made home bakes. There's also a lovely chapel just along the road from there which has a special atmosphere, and a beautifully crafted wooden ceiling which reminds me of the inside of an upturned boat."

Getting to Scotland from central London has never been easier

With a minimum check-in time of only 15 minutes with hand luggage, British Airways offers you a quicker way to travel from central London to Scotland, so that you can maximise your time exploring your chosen destination.

There are 11 flights every weekday between London City Airport and Scotland - 7 to Edinburgh and 4 to Glasgow - therefore it's never been easier to find the perfect flight.

We offer free seat assignment within 24 hours of your flight via online check-in, plus complimentary snacks and drinks on board all our flights, as well as 1 piece of free checked in luggage.

Step onto our new aircraft and discover the most comfortable flight experience, with only 2 seats either side of the aisle. That means no middle seat and up to 33" of legroom. So stretch out those legs, sit back and relax in style!

For flight times and further information, go to: visitscotland.com/ba

1.

BRITISH AIRWAYS
London City

1. NEW BRITISH AIRWAYS FLEET
2. EDINBURGH CASTLE, EDINBURGH
3. KELVINGROVE ART GALLERY AND MUSEUM, GLASGOW

1. TWO OF THE THREE SISTERS, GLEN COE, HIGHLANDS

2. THE WEST HIGHLAND LINE, GLENFINNAN VIADUCT AND LOCH SHIEL, HIGHLANDS

3. LOCH LAGGAN, HIGHLANDS

4. LOCH TORRIDON, HIGHLANDS

5. HEADSTONE OF THE CLAN MACKINTOSH, CULLODEN BATTLEFIELD, HIGHLANDS

THE HIGHLANDS

The magnificently sprawling Highlands offer you the chance to visit one of the last really wild places in Scotland and one of the most dramatic landscapes in Europe. Witness the remarkable wildlife and participate in thrilling outdoor activities. Explore the majestic mountains and beautiful glens, romantic islands and stunning stretches of coastline, or feast on fresh seafood and follow the history of Scotland's Malt Whisky Trail. Whatever you decide to do, the Highlands reward time and again.

Marvel at the sheer scale of the Torridon hills or take on the challenging wilderness of Knoydart. Be amazed by the interlaced lochans of the Flow Country in Caithness and the sandstone peaks of Inverpolly and Coigach. In the north, find deep forests, dramatic cliffs, ragged peaks and tumultuous seas crashing together. And in the south, delve into the history of gruesome clan battles whilst discovering the true crossroads of the Scottish Highlands at Glen Spean and the Great Glen. The list is endless and truly a lifetime's exploration.

The history of the Highlands is visible in its landscape with

5.

famous battlefields like Culloden, striking Pictish stones and historic forts. It is a very evocative region of Scotland and as well as admiring the scenery, it is worth appreciating the history as you travel through 5,000 years of its Pictish, Viking, and Gaelic past.

6.

7.

8.

The Highlands are noted for their venison, from red deer rather than from the lowland roe. This is what to do with a large haunch or saddle.

Highland Venison Recipe

MARINADE

Prepare a marinade with a bottle of red wine, bay leaves, garlic, black peppercorns, sprig of rosemary, crushed juniper berries, and olive oil. Add 2 carrots and an onion and soak the meat for 2 days.

COOKING METHOD

When ready, in a large pan fry diced bacon and then add the haunch, browning on all sides. Add the marinade and boil to reduce by half. Season then place in the oven, cooking at 180°C for 60 minutes per kilo. After cooking the joint, make a sauce with the pan juices, reducing again on the stove, and adding a tbsp of flour with a tbsp of butter, rubbed together. Add around half a cup of port and a tbsp of rowan jelly, mixing everything well.

INGREDIENTS

Haunch of venison
Bacon
Bottle of red wine
Bay leaves
Garlic
Black peppercorns
Sprig of rosemary
Juniper berries
Olive oil
2 Carrots
1 Onion

Tbsp Flour
Tbsp Butter
Tbsp Rowan jelly
1/2 Cup Port

The Highlands is the perfect base for touring not only the most popular, but also the less well known areas of Scotland that few people get to see. However, like the landscape, the roads themselves vary. For example, Ullapool and the breathtaking western seaboard

6. OLD PACKHORSE BRIDGE, RIVER OF DULNAIN, CARRBRIDGE, HIGHLANDS

7. BEN LOYAL, NEAR TONGUE, HIGHLANDS

8. LOCH GARRY, WEST OF INVERGARRY, HIGHLANDS

9. STAC POLLY, INVERPOLLY NATIONAL NATURE RESERVE, HIGHLANDS

10. LOCH TORRIDON, TORRIDON, HIGHLANDS

9.

10.

are little over an hour's drive from Inverness. In contrast, there are still a few places where you will encounter single track roads: for instance, around the far north west corner in Ardnamurchan; Bealach na Ba, by Applecross (one of the highest roads in Britain) and in Glen Torridon. These are superbly scenic areas, where you can relax and soak up the delights and contrast of rugged mountains and spacious wilderness, of thrilling coastal roads and wildlife-filled cross country drives.

Bear in mind that other road users may be in more of a rush than you, so be polite when it comes to allowing faster traffic to overtake by using the passing places.

Hidden Gem

An Lochan Uaine, Glenmore.

There are many walks in the area around Aviemore, especially in the old pinewoods that cover the Cairngorm foothills around Rothiemurchus and Abernethy Forest. Some of these tracks lead into the heart of the mountain wilderness. On the way to Strath Nethy, north west of Glenmore Lodge one route goes past An Lochan Uaine - the 'little green loch'. It's worth pausing here, as it really is green - under certain lights a quite unnatural blue-green. A trick of the light or the colour of the sandy bed below it? It's well worth the walk to check it out.

Myths & Legends

One of the best known of all the mythological beasts of the Highlands, the kelpie, was definitely not to be trusted. The water-horse - Gaelic 'each-uisge' - was inclined to hang about riverbanks tempting riders on to its back, at which point it would plunge into the water. Even today, there are a few lochs named on OS maps 'Lochan na Beiste' - loch of the beast.

Come and try to spot the most famous beast of them all - the Loch Ness Monster.

FACT

What makes the landscape of the north west unique is its geology. The Lewisian Gneiss that forms the base of many of the mountains of Sutherland is the oldest rock in the UK - a mind blowing 3,000 million years. On top of this plinth of ancient rock sit peaks like Stac Polly, Suilven, Quinag and Ben More Coigach - far from the highest in Scotland but with spectacular profiles. These are all that is left of younger sandstone rocks that have been carved away by erosion. Explore this further at Knockan Crag, by the road north of Ullapool, within the North West Highlands Geopark, a status granted by UNESCO in 2004.

Tell your friends when you get back

The last community of any size in the far north west is Durness, quite near Cape Wrath. It's a beautiful stark area, with a superb rugged coastline and is about the last place you would expect a John Lennon Memorial Garden. But there is one. Lennon spent several summers here in his boyhood at his cousins' family's croft house in Sangomore.

Historical Fact

The potato famine of the 1840s affected the Highlands of Scotland so badly a variety of relief programmes were put in place. One scheme involved the Government and the lairds employing local crofters to build roads, which aimed to improve communications and increase value of the estates in Scotland. To avoid a dependency culture the starving local folk were paid in meals for their work on the new roads. That is why today, a section of the A832, between Little Loch Broom and Loch Broom, across a wide moor with magnificent views, is still known as Destitution Road.

11. DUN TELVE, ONE OF THE GLENELG
   BROCHS, HIGHLANDS

11.

Real People Tips

After a career in the army, Alastair
Cunningham went into the travel
business, arranging tailored
holidays to Scottish castles and
clan lands. He reckons the ideal
off-the-beaten-track place is Glenelg, reached by
a memorably twisting road with sensational views. "It's a tiny west coast
community, home to the best preserved Iron Age brochs on the mainland, an
old-fashioned turntable ferry to the Isle of Skye and a great road to nowhere."

Hints & Tips

Some maps mark the
Portnancon Souterrain - an Iron
Age food store (some say). It's
quite easy to find near the road
but requiring a bit more effort to
find is a fascinating wheelhouse
in the rough moorland to the
west of Loch Eriboll. This is
another Iron Age site, this time
a circular dwelling, still partly
roofed. Take a walk into the
wild setting, north west from
Portnancon, just for the sheer
atmosphere. Bring your walking
boots!

SCRABSTER
DURNESS   THURSO   JOHN
               O'GROATS
PORTNANCON   CAITHNESS   WICK

ULLAPOOL

DINGWALL
               CULLODEN
          INVERNESS

          AVIEMORE
KNOYDART   Cairngorms
                         National Par
MALLAIG
          FORT WILLIAM

THE CITIES

Each of Scotland's six cities have a distinctive character of their own, but all guarantee visitors a sophisticated urban experience with a vibrant mix of history, culture and entertainment, stirred together with some of the best retail therapy in the UK.

Glasgow is Scotland with style. It's a blend of internationally acclaimed museums and galleries, stunning architecture, vibrant nightlife, fabulous shopping, unmatched wining and dining options and vast cultural choice including the world famous Kelvingrove Art Gallery and Museum, home to one of the UK's finest civic art collections. And with more than 120 separate music events taking place each week, Glasgow has been recognised as a UNESCO City of Music.

2.

1.

In contrast, the capital of Scotland, Edinburgh is a UNESCO City of Literature. A city that inspired writers from the time of the medieval Scots 'makars' or poets right through to the birthplace of Sir Walter Scott. It's one of Europe's great capital cities, a place where history and natural beauty combine to provide a feast for the eyes and the mind.

1. GLASGOW SCHOOL OF ART, GLASGOW
2. KELVINGROVE ART GALLERY AND MUSEUM, GLASGOW
3. THE TOWN HOUSE, ABERDEEN
4. THE FORTH RAIL BRIDGE, SOUTH QUEENSFERRY, NEAR EDINBURGH
5. ST CUTHBERT'S PARISH CHURCH BELOW EDINBURGH CASTLE, EDINBURGH

Explore grand historic royal palaces and elegant shopping arcades, or take in a show in the world's 'Festival City' before indulging in the city's fabulously varied dining experiences.

third largest city offers a host of treasures waiting to be explored.

Meanwhile, Dundee, like Glasgow, successfully rebranded itself as a post-industrial city. As 'One City, Many Discoveries', Dundee has a long-standing history of innovation. Be it X-ray techniques or electric light in the 1800s to more modern developments such as computer gaming, the city's innovators have pioneered throughout the years, and continue to push the boundaries.

6.

7.

8.

Popular attractions include the recently refurbished McManus: Dundee's Art Gallery and Museum, Discovery Point, and Dundee Contemporary Arts as a flagship cultural venue.

Aberdeen is different again; its long promenade helped it formerly earn the description of 'Scotland's largest seaside resort', but it's much more than that. Fusing striking granite architecture, a rich and inspiring history that can be seen in attractions such as the 5-star Aberdeen Maritime Museum, a dynamic modern arts scene, and perhaps Scotland's strongest industrial heritage, the country's

As part of the Millennium celebrations, Inverness, capital of the Highlands, joined the ranks of Scotland's cities. Quite right, as this major commercial centre is certainly no quaint Highland community, but a lively place with a thriving culture and nightlife.

Hints & Tips

Born in 1868, Charles Rennie Mackintosh is to this day regarded as the father of Glasgow Style. Fascinating attractions, such as House for an Art Lover and Glasgow School of Art, are dotted throughout the city telling the story of Glasgow's famous architect as well as displaying his unique style. Talking of style, nobody would deny that Glasgow has the widest choice of shops in Scotland and in fact in the rest of the UK only coming second to London. The Argyll Arcade was the first custom built shopping arcade in Scotland, opening in 1827. All the top names are in town at places like the Buchanan Galleries and the stunning Princes Square. But for enterprise, exclusivity and a few surprises, it still has to be the Merchant City.

6. THE EDINBURGH MILITARY TATTOO, EDINBURGH

7. THE CASTLEGATE, ABERDEEN

8. RRS DISCOVERY AT DISCOVERY POINT, DUNDEE

FACT

A visit to Stirling Castle is a must, for a glimpse of life at Scotland's royal court in the 16th century, before King James VI went south at the Union of the Crowns in 1603 and changed Scotland's history. For example, King James V sought light relief from his European machinations and revenue earning activities on the home front by disguising himself as a poor farmer. He would slip out from the castle by a side door at Ballengeich, between the Castle Rock and the Gowanhill on the east side of the ramparts, and he would wander about among his subjects, discoursing with beggars and travellers. He would also dally - and worse - with country lasses. The disguised King, gathering intelligence, was known as the 'Guidman o' Ballengeich'. He died, aged only 30, in 1542. His only surviving legitimate child was also prominent in Scotland's affairs: Mary Queen of Scots.

Real People Tips

Wilma Paterson lives in Tayport, opposite Dundee on the Firth of Tay. She's a travel writer, composer and a member of the British Guild of Travel Writers and Society of Authors. "Eating out in Dundee", she says, "usually means the DCA - Dundee Contemporary Arts - which is a really pleasant, civilised place for lunch or dinner (or a coffee or pre-cinema drink). I like the ambience and it's great for people of all ages. I also like The Rep - Dundee Repertory Theatre - in Tay Square for a pre-theatre meal. The Phoenix Bar (in Nethergate) is my favourite pub in Dundee. It has an old-fashioned lively pub atmosphere and the staff are really nice and friendly. You get lots of art students from Duncan of Jordanstone and the university, and journalists from DC Thomson congregate there after work. It's great value and portions are very hearty!"

With its suspension bridges across the River Ness to the lovely Ness Islands, and the city's old stone buildings, it is a pretty place to explore and is lavishly decorated with flowers.

Wars of Independence were fought and won here, so, although this is Scotland's newest city, it is truly alive with history and heritage.

Six cities, offering six very different experiences of Scotland.

9.

11.

10.

Stirling followed on, gaining city status in 2002. Meander through the Old Town and feel the sense of history, then take in the views of seven battlefields including Bannockburn from Stirling Castle. This stunning cliff-top castle is where monarchs ruled in regal splendour and where merchants and craftsmen plied their trade below the castle rock.

Tell your friends when you get back

Officially speaking, a city isn't just a very large town, or a place with a cathedral. In Scotland and the rest of the UK, only the reigning monarch and ministers can grant city status. They hold a competition, and the aspiring towns have to meet certain criteria. The newest city in Scotland is Stirling, only since 2002. Inverness got its status in 2000. Perth, sometimes known as 'the Fair City' has high hopes for official status in the next competition.

9. INVERNESS CASTLE, HIGHLANDS
10. STIRLING CASTLE, STIRLING
11. 'THE FAIR CITY' OF PERTH AND THE RIVER TAY

FACT

Downtown landmarks in Inverness include the Tolbooth Steeple's spire of 1791, which had to be repaired after an earth tremor of all things in 1816. Opposite is the Town House. It was here in 1921 that Lloyd George, then Prime Minister, held the first ever Cabinet meeting outside London.

The Aberdeen Buttery

Aberdeen is the home of the buttery, aka the buttery rowie, or plain rowie or even just roll. Sometimes described as the first cousin of the French croissant, butteries seldom survive the transition to the central belt of Scotland and become pale imitations of the real thing. The finest are still to be found in a few city bakers and also in the village of Rhynie. Their high fat content was meant to give them good keeping qualities as they were formerly taken to sea as sustenance for fishermen. If you find one offered at breakfast in an Aberdeen hotel, ask your waiter or waitress to pop it into the toaster and serve warm.

Hints & Tips

Think that Edinburgh's Royal Mile is looking busy? There are ways of finding a peaceful spot. First of all, you could take a tour that leads you through the hidden gardens around these historic streets. Check out Green Yonder Tours. Or perhaps you just need a nice cup of tea? The Scottish Storytelling Centre on the Royal Mile has a lovely garden at the back. Often not as busy as other places nearby. Then there is St Giles' Cathedral Café, tucked downstairs at the back of St Giles' Cathedral off the High Street, offering great food and most importantly, it's hidden away.

1. THE OLD COURSE,
    ST ANDREWS, FIFE
2. THE RIVER DEE, NEAR
    BALLATER, ABERDEENSHIRE
3. THE BEACH AT ST CYRUS,
    ABERDEENSHIRE
4. LOCH TAY, PERTHSHIRE
5. THE HARBOUR, CRAIL, FIFE

THE EAST

This is classic Scotland, where coast and glen combine bringing together the best of the country's landscapes. The wild upland scenery of the western parts of Perthshire, Angus and Aberdeenshire are a great feature of the area, but the true heart of the region is in the lowland prosperity with the rich farmlands around the market towns and coastal communities, surrounded by the beautiful sea.

In fact, from the East Neuk of Fife fishing villages all the way round the vast shoreline to the Moray Firth coast by Banff and Portsoy, you can see fishing has left its mark. There are now active and modernised fishing ports, especially on the north east knuckle of Scotland, but you can still find quaint and photogenic little harbours, such as Crail in Fife.

4.

5.

Between the coast and high ground, lies a band of rich farmland, where meat and dairy produce makes for fantastic local cooking - Aberdeen Angus beef and seafood can usually be found on most menus. Then there is the soft fruit, the game, plus the most northerly crop of asparagus, grown in Strathmore. In short, you will be able to eat well here!

6.

7.

Amongst the high ground, towns such as Crieff or Dunkeld in Perthshire, Kirriemuir in Angus, or Ballater in Aberdeenshire, all feel like a portal - a crossing place from the rich lowlands into the stunning highlands. This is why the area is most appealing, as you can experience both sides of Scotland, by travelling from the quayside to the high mountain tops.

Tell your friends when you get back

All the castles across Scotland are loved for their beauty, but for the best in sheer quality and variety, the Castles of Mar are well worth visiting on the waymarked Castle Trail in Aberdeenshire. Visitors to the castles are generally astounded by their great state of preservation due to their location - Aberdeenshire lies beyond the Grampian mountains, out of the way of some of the battles and marauding armies of the olden days. Many of the castles still stand just as their builders left them. Take beautiful Craigievar, for example, rumoured to be the inspiration for the Walt Disney logo.

Wildlife Tip

St Cyrus is a National Nature Reserve, just to the north of Montrose. To the south is another nature reserve: Montrose Basin. While that one is all about wild geese and ducks in the breezy tidal estuary, St Cyrus is gentler and even more picturesque, with golden sands, wildflowers galore in the grasslands and verdant cliffs. Botanists find it of special interest as it is a place where some northern species reach their southerly limit.

The heritage of the three important elements of the east of Scotland, coast, farmland, and mountain, can all be explored in a good range of local museums. As well as the Scottish Fisheries Museum at Anstruther in Fife, there is another maritime themed collection at the Museum of Scottish Lighthouses in Fraserburgh.

6. WOODLAND AT THE HERMITAGE, NEAR DUNKELD, PERTH AND KINROSS

7. CRAIGIEVAR CASTLE, KINTOCHER, ABERDEENSHIRE

8. THE HARBOUR, ST MONANS, FIFE

9. GLEN DOLL, ANGUS

8.

9.

The Angus Folk Museum at Glamis and the Aberdeenshire Farming Museum at Mintlaw give real insight into the lives of the farming folk who made a living from the once poor ground, which has now been transformed by the work of generations into some of

Hints & Tips

For a relaxing day out and some delicious, authentic food, visit Charleton Fruit Farm, just north of Montrose. Spend a few hours picking your own berries before visiting the coffee shop in the converted old stable blocks. Enjoy a cup of coffee or tea and one of the farm's famous strawberry tarts - a delicious fruity treat.

Hidden Gem

Kingarrock Golf Course, The Kingdom of Fife.

Golf enthusiasts know that The Kingdom of Fife is home to many challenging and beautiful courses including the Old Course at St Andrews which hosts The Open Championship every five years. What is less known perhaps, is just 10 miles from this famous course is Kingarrock, at which you can feel the thrill of the game from 100 years ago as you play this 9-hole course with hickory shafts! Staffed by people knowledgeable in the period 1910 -1930, they will provide tips on how to use the spoon, driving iron, mashie, niblick and putter!

Scotland's finest farmlands. This is a theme taken up by one of the area's best-known writers, Lewis Grassic Gibbon, whose classic 'Sunset Song' is a vivid evocation of the toil of farming life. Find out more about him in the heart of the Mearns countryside, at the Grassic Gibbon Centre in the small village of Arbuthnott. Meanwhile, discover a real insight into life in the glens at the Glenesk Folk Museum, hidden high in one of the Angus Glens.

Take in the sights of this land from the many viewpoints such as the Cairn o' Mount, between Fettercairn and Banchory, which brings home the essence of the east - spot the low grounds of Fife with a distant glint of beaches, the Angus farming country of Strathmore and, on the other side, the high moors that roll out to the big hills westwards. It's just another of Scotland's great panoramas.

10.

11.

Hints & Tips

The bottlenose dolphins of the Moray Firth are the largest examples of the species in the world because the rich feeding grounds allow them to develop an extra thick layer of blubber. As well as the inner Moray Firth, they can turn up anywhere on the north-facing part of the Aberdeenshire coastline. Portsoy, Macduff and New Aberdour are all good places to spot them, or they can even be seen from the windows of the café at the Museum of Scottish Lighthouses, right at the tip of Kinnaird Head, where the Moray Firth turns into the North Sea. There's a great beach here too.

Hints & Tips

Perthshire is known as Big Tree Country and a visit to Cluny House Gardens by Aberfeldy will make you understand how this region gets this name. Planted in 1950 by Bobby and Betty Masterton, the gardens feature trees and shrubs from America, New Zealand, Japan, China and Tibet merged with native plants to create the unique atmosphere of a Himalayan woodland paradise.

FACT

Scotland is home to around 121,000 red squirrels, about 75% of the entire UK population. Look out for them when you're walking in the woods below Bennachie, the landmark hill range in Aberdeenshire, near Inverurie, and also in the woods by Crathes Castle near Banchory. In other parts of Scotland, such as the Crieff area of Perthshire, look out for the red squirrels, who are retreating before the spread of the non-native grey.

10. LOOKING OVER THE MONTROSE BASIN, ANGUS
11. CLUNY HOUSE GARDENS, NEAR ABERFELDY, PERTHSHIRE

PORTSOY FRASERBURGH
BANFF
MINTLAW
KINTOCHER
ABERDEEN
Cairngorms National Park
BALLATER
MONTROSE
KIRRIEMUIR
DUNKELD GLAMIS
ARBROATH
CRIEFF PERTH DUNDEE
ST ANDREWS
CRAIL
ANSTRUTHER
KINROSS
DUNFERMLINE
EDINBURGH

Local Dish
Arbroath Smokies

Arbroath Smokies come exclusively from this north east fishing town, where they are still produced using similar methods as in the 18th century. The haddock is dry salted in tubs to draw excess moisture from the fish and toughen the skin in preparation for the smoking process. The sticks of fish are then placed over a smokie pit - a half whisky barrel, set into the ground and lined with slates to protect it, with a hardwood fire of beech and oak. The cooking time is usually a minimum of 30 to 40 minutes, but only an experienced smokie maker knows exactly when it is ready. The beautiful golden brown fish can be eaten straight from the barrel and you can enjoy the truly mouth-watering experience at restaurants throughout the area or buy straight from the makers in Arbroath. In 2004, the European Commission registered the designation 'Arbroath Smokies' as a Protected Geographical Indication under the EU's Protected Food Name Scheme, acknowledging its unique status.

THE WEST

Scotland's lochs, woodlands, hills, and ruined castles suited the taste of early tourists in the Romantic Age, just before the end of the 18th century. You can still capture their idea of romantic landscapes in The Trossachs, Loch Lomond, and Argyll, which embody much of what makes Scotland so attractive.

2.

Loch Lomond and The Trossachs National Park was the first of its kind created in Scotland - a shining jewel at the centre of the Scottish Heartlands - while the cities of Edinburgh, Glasgow and Stirling are surprisingly close, considering the tranquillity on offer.

What could be more Scottish than ruined Kilchurn Castle on its headland by Loch Awe? Or those sunsets over the islands you see from the roads down the Kintyre Peninsula, south of Oban?

The long fingers of the scenic sea lochs can lengthen journey times in the west but just one interesting way into Argyll is to take the Gourock to Dunoon ferry, shortening journey times to the beauties of Cowal.

1.

1. LOCH TULLA, ARGYLL
2. VIEW OF LOCH LOMOND
3. PATH UP 'THE COBBLER', LOCH LOMOND NATIONAL PARK
4. ROWARDENNAN, LOCH LOMOND
5. KILCHURN CASTLE, LOCH AWE, ARGYLL

3.

4.

5.

This area of Scotland appeals to a whole spectrum of visitors. It's great for little adventures such as fast RIB boat trips off the western seaboard. Towering peaks make places like Crianlarich, on the West Highland Way, a favourite with Munro baggers, while Rannoch Moor lies nearby as well.

7.

6.

There are also plenty of gentler pursuits. Kilmartin Glen is a peaceful retreat where you can mull over the meaning of the unique standing stones and cairns. Breathtaking views of Islay and Jura can be enjoyed from the Kintyre Peninsula and Knapdale is the perfect place to spot wildcats or even beavers.

Equally, you can enjoy the unique stir and bustle that is Oban in high season. This Gateway to the Isles is alive with an exciting sense of departure as visitors hop aboard ferries to the magical Hebridean Isles.

FACT

Doune Castle, west of Stirling, was built in the 14th century by the powerful Regent of Scotland, Robert Stewart, Duke of Albany. It's the best example of a medieval fortress surviving in Scotland, and became even more famous for its role in Monty Python and the Holy Grail. Look closely on your visit to see how important security was. The main halls each have their own access stairs to aid defence. The Lord's hall allows operation of the portcullis immediately below - while the Duke's bedroom has an emergency exit. Other notable features include the kitchen with its 18ft wide fireplace. Its heat also warmed guest bedrooms immediately above - an early example of under floor heating.

6.   A SCOTTISH WILDCAT

7.   DOUNE CASTLE,
     SOUTH OF DOUNE, STIRLING

8.   ST COLUMBA'S FOOTPRINTS,
     MULL OF KINTYRE, ARGYLL

Folklore

Callander is a bustling town, which marks the gateway to The Trossachs. Just north of here, Ben Ledi is a very popular mountain climb and for generations it was associated with Beltane rituals. In Gaelic society, Beltane was celebrated on the 1st May and signified the moving of herds up to high summer pastures. Young people would gather on moorland, build fires, and bake oatcakes. Today, in an echo of this old practice, some head for the summit not on May Day but on the late evening of Midsummer Day. The sun sets at its furthest point north, in a notch between the mountains of Ben More and Stobinian.

Hints & Tips

For the best view of Loch Lomond, stroll up Duncryne hill (known locally as The Dumpling), south of Gartocharn. For its size - only 470ft (142m) high - it offers a magnificent panorama making the climb well worth it. This volcanic plug is an eye-catching geology lesson too. You can contemplate how, at the end of the last Ice Age, a glacier coming down from the north melted here and deposited enough material to create a natural dam, so that the Loch Lomond surface is only 27ft (8m) above sea level. The 'bonnie banks' almost became a sea-loch, like Loch Long, a little way to the west.

Myths & Legends

Footprints carved into the rock are a mysterious feature at Dunadd and they also appear on top of a rock near Southend by the Mull of Kintyre. Some say these were linked to 'King-making' ceremonies, although over time the Southend carvings came to be associated with St Columba as well. He landed here in 563AD, exiled from Ireland, but sailed on to Iona where he began to spread the word of Christianity throughout Scotland. St Columba's Chapel lies within Keil Cemetery, at the southern tip of the Kintyre Peninsula. Today, the footprints are signposted from the road, and there are also signposted caves nearby to view.

8.

Tell your friends when you get back

Oban has always been a busy west Highland destination and ferry port - ever since Victorian times when the local folk refused to let the railway come into town via the seafront in case it spoilt their views from the promenade. There's still a rail link today. However, it's the choice of seafood restaurants that seems to have put Oban on the map for foodies. Also in Argyll, time it right and you can enjoy the annual Tarbert Seafood Festival, held on the first weekend in July.

10.

FACT

In the heart of The Trossachs, Loch Katrine's clear waters provide a water supply to the city of Glasgow. The massive engineering project to bring clean supplies to the city started in 1855. Four years later, Queen Victoria opened the 26 mile long tunnel and aqueduct. To see something of the engineering, follow a path at the back of Loch Chon, on the Stronachlachar road. Various mysterious looking shafts and iron structures are hidden by the trees near the loch.

Hints & Tips

The Falls of Lora are below the Connel Bridge near Oban. They are not always seen, as they are a tidal confluence caused by the mass of water from Loch Etive meeting the incoming sea. Time it right, however, and it can be quite spectacular. Look for the viewpoint car park west of the bridge, close to the Oyster Inn.

9.

Real People Tips

Cameron Taylor runs Portnellan self-catering holiday accommodation near Crianlarich and having lived in Glen Dochart for most of his life, he can offer visitors plenty of local gems to explore. As a cyclist, he especially likes the circuit that takes in Glen Orchy, west of Tyndrum. His favourite walk is into the hills behind Kenknock Farm, far up Glen Lochay.

Hints & Tips

The area around Kilmartin Glen in Argyll has lots of ancient sites such as cairns and stone circles - basically, it's one of mainland Scotland's richest prehistoric landscapes. The Kilmartin House Museum tells the story and whilst here, you should also visit the Glebe Cairn Café, which has a great reputation built on its imaginative and flexible menus. A little way to the south is Dunadd, a hilltop fort formerly surrounded by boggy ground (now fields). This was the ancient capital of Dalriada, the first Kingdom of the Scots.

9. CONNEL BRIDGE AND LOCH ETIVE, NEAR OBAN, ARGYLL

10. LOCH CHON, STIRLING DISTRICT

11. STANDING STONES, NEAR KILMARTIN, ARGYLL

11.

1.

2.

3.

4.

1. SCOTT'S VIEW, NEAR MELROSE, SCOTTISH BORDERS

2. CULZEAN CASTLE, SOUTH AYRSHIRE

3. JEDBURGH ABBEY, SCOTTISH BORDERS

4. LOCH TROOL, DUMFRIES & GALLOWAY

5. SMAILHOLM TOWER, SMAILHOLM, SCOTTISH BORDERS

6. HUME CASTLE, SCOTTISH BORDERS

THE SOUTH

The Scottish experience starts at the border. It's quite subtle, but listen and you will hear the accents are different, as are the names of the beers in the local pub.

The Scottish Borders is a place to let your imagination break free. A speciality of the area are the viewpoints. Stand on the battlements of Hume Castle near Greenlaw; take in the panorama from Smailholm Tower near Melrose, or the famous Scott's View of the Eildons. Gaze out to

6.

5.

the blue rolling hills and, in your mind's eye at least, you can see the distant glint of the armour of an approaching army. Actually, no, it's probably just a tractor, but that is the magic of these borderlands.

To the west, in Galloway, dramatic hills roll down to pasture with dark woods that, in turn, give way to rich farmlands and a sunny south facing coast.

Once a bustling port, charming Kirkcudbright (pronounced 'kir-coo-bree') is now a tranquil, well-preserved little 18th and early 19th century town with a rich artistic heritage just waiting to be explored.

Northwards, the Galloway moors run into Ayrshire, the birthplace of Robert Burns. As well as a whole range of places associated with Scotland's national poet, Ayrshire is a golfer's delight, and has plenty of 'must sees', notably Culzean Castle, one of the most popular properties belonging to the National Trust for Scotland.

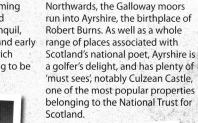

7.

9.

8.

FACT

Ayrshire and the Clyde coast seem to have been made for golf courses - The Open Championship was born at Prestwick Golf Club in 1860.

Real People Tips

As a full-time travel writer and main contributor to guides by many major publishers, Moniaive resident Hugh Taylor should know about where to eat. "The Green Tea House in Moniaive is not only my favourite local restaurant but my favourite place to eat in all of the world. It's run by Catherine Braid, an imaginative and innovative cook on fair trade and green policies and the standard of the food and service is just amazing. During Moniaive Folk Festival she opens round the clock for the weekend and the place is jam-packed with musicians."

The south is overflowing with things to do. The mild air of the Gulf Stream promotes all manner of outdoor pursuits, from walking a cross-section of the Southern Upland Way or visiting a 7stanes centre for some mountain biking, to simply exploring fabulous gardens and historic sites such as Caerlaverock Castle, one of the finest medieval castles in Scotland.

In short, plenty to see, lots to do and a network of rural roads so you can really take your time. It's all very relaxing in the south of Scotland.

Tell your friends when you get back

You would think the highest village in Scotland would be in the Highlands - but no, it's Wanlockhead in the Southern Uplands, at 1531ft (466m). This is in an area where some of the world's purest gold (22.8 carat) was found. That gold formed part of the Scottish Regalia. However, Wanlockhead became more closely associated with lead mining. The Scottish Museum of Lead Mining is here today.

10.

Fact & Tip

If you are exploring the Mull of Galloway, is it worth going all the way to the end, to the very tip? Most definitely. For a start, you can then say you've been to the most southerly part of Scotland. Secondly, the views are superb. The lighthouse there was built by Robert Stevenson in 1830. Thirdly, if the wind is blowing, then you can warm up with a coffee at the Gallie Craig cliff-top coffee house, tucked into the lee of the headland but still giving great views.

7. GALLOWAY FOREST PARK, LOCH KEN, DUMFRIES & GALLOWAY

8. BURNS' COTTAGE, ALLOWAY, AYRSHIRE

9. PRESTWICK GOLF CLUB, AYRSHIRE

10. CAERLAVEROCK CASTLE, DUMFRIES & GALLOWAY

At places like the Grey Mare's Tail, spectacular scenery carved by ancient glaciers create a landscape every bit as impressive as the Highlands to the north. And much the same can be said for Glen Trool, further west.

13.

11.

Furthermore, if you explore, say, the countryside behind the old fishing port of Girvan, perhaps following the River Stinchar, then up there, off-the-beaten-track, with woodlands, rippling waters and a ruined castle or two - well, you'll feel as though you've stepped in to some romantic Victorian oil painting.

Proof, if it were needed, of the beauty of these uplands and this inspirational setting, is in the thriving arts scene - Galloway's Spring Fling is just one of the hugely successful events in the cultural calendar.

12.

11. THE GREY MARE'S TAIL, NEAR MOFFAT, DUMFRIES & GALLOWAY

12. THE RUINS OF SWEETHEART ABBEY, DUMFRIES & GALLOWAY

13. GIRVAN HARBOUR, SOUTH AYRSHIRE

Hints & Tips

Woodside Walled Garden north of Jedburgh off the A68 is where you find lots of local folk getting top tips for growing fruit and vegetables in their own garden, and enjoying lunch in the café. There's a wildlife garden as well and birdlife thrives. Lucky visitors will get a table right at the wildlife viewing window. However, the closed-circuit TV in the nuthatch nest box means everyone sees something.

Hints & Tips

The Borders Abbeys Way is a circular walking route linking the four great ruined abbeys situated in Kelso, Jedburgh, Melrose and Dryburgh. As well as admiring these stunning pieces of history, the 64 mile route will also take you through the wonderful Borders countryside of rounded green hills, wooded riverbanks, pine-scented forests and rich farmland.

Hidden Gem

Striding Arches, Glenkiln, Dumfries.

Andy Goldsworthy is one of the world's foremost artists working directly in the landscape. Striding Arches is the first of Goldsworthy's large-scale projects involving multiple structures to be installed in a public landscape in Scotland. This is a hugely innovative artist-led project which celebrates Dumfries & Galloway with the red sandstone arch 'striding' around the natural amphitheatre that is Cairnhead.

1. TOURING BEAUTIFUL SCOTLAND
2. LOCH MAREE, WESTER ROSS
3. BRUERNISH, ISLE OF BARRA

Images used are for illustrative purposes only and may not represent actual vehicle for hire.

FAMOUS SCOTS

Scots in History & Hollywood

Famous Scots from history have inspired films. The story of **Sir William Wallace (1272-1305)** was loosely told in the Oscar-winning movie Braveheart. **Mary of Scotland (1936)**, saw *Katharine Hepburn* playing Mary Queen of Scots, and **Bonnie Prince Charlie (1948)** starred *David Niven* (somewhat unconvincingly). More recently it was **Rob Roy** with *Liam Neeson* that saw another historically famous Scot given the Hollywood treatment. **Rob Roy MacGregor (1671-1734)**, cattle dealer, protection racket operator and sometime Jacobite supporter, witnessed some of the most important events in a turbulent episode in Scotland's story, yet survived to die peacefully at home in Balquhidder. People still visit his grave today.

1.

2.

3.

More Scots on the Silver Screen

Everyone knows about *Sir Sean Connery*, who, before success, earned extra money as a young man by posing as a model in Edinburgh College of Art. But other Scots have sought fame on stage and the silver screen. *Dougray Scott* was born in 1965 in Glenrothes in Fife. *Alan Cumming* was born in the same year in Aberfeldy and brought up in Angus. *Gerard Butler* was born in Paisley in 1969 and trained as a lawyer before becoming an actor. And Crieff's most famous son is surely *Ewan McGregor*, born in 1971.

Scots in Science

Alexander Graham Bell (1847-1922): Born in South Charlotte Street, Edinburgh. Inventor of the telephone.

John Logie Baird (1888-1946): Born in Helensburgh. Invented television, using a mechanical system soon superseded.

4.

John Napier (1550-1617): Born in Merchiston Castle, Edinburgh. Invented logarithms (amongst many other mathematical concepts, including the point in the decimal fraction!) and with his design for a 'burning mirror,' may have foreseen the laser.

James Young (1811-1883): Glasgow born industrial chemist, known as 'Paraffin Young', first produced oil commercially.

James Clerk Maxwell (1831-1879): Son of a Dunfermline landowner, now recognised as second to Einstein and Newton in his contribution to science. He also took the first ever colour photograph.

1. THE WALLACE MONUMENT, STIRLING
2. STATUE OF SIR WILLIAM WALLACE, ABERDEEN
3. GRAVE OF ROB ROY MACGREGOR, BALQUHIDDER
4. VIEW ACROSS CHARLOTTE SQUARE, EDINBURGH

More Famous Scots

Some gave their names to land features in far-off shores: such as the **Pitcairn Islands** off Australia or Canada's **Mackenzie River**. Others invented the means of getting around: The first pedal powered bicycle was invented by **Kirkpatrick Macmillan** in 1839. The first practical steamboat in the UK was designed by **William Symington (1764-1831)**. It sailed on Dalswinton Loch near Dumfries, on an estate owned by Patrick Miller, who was Robert Burns' landlord at the time. Some say Burns had a trip on the boat. Around the same time, Angus-born **James Tytler** took off in a balloon and became the first person in the UK to leave the ground in 1784.

Scots in the Kitchen Cupboard

Dundee Marmalade was created by **Mrs Janet Keiller** of Dundee, 1797. Her son founded Keiller & Co., and the preserve became famous worldwide. 'Canada Dry' was invented by Scottish chemist, **John McLaughlin** in Toronto, 1890. Rose's lime juice is named after its inventor, **Lachlan Rose**, who marketed the first branded fruit juice. Meanwhile, **John Polson** put his name to cornflour and **John Lawson Johnston** invented Bovril. Johnston was an Edinburgh butcher who originally called his product 'Johnston's Fluid Beef.' Through its success he became very wealthy and lived in a grand house known as Bovril Castle.

But not all inventions were world-changing. The first ever recorded steam tricycle was designed and used by an Aberdeenshire postman **Andrew Lawson** in 1895. It was known as the Craigievar Express. This was not taken up by Royal Mail - but you can actually see the machine in the Grampian Transport Museum in Alford today.

Scots in sport like **Sir Chris Hoy**, in music and culture, for example, **Nicola Benedetti**, and in popular entertainment - high profile **Susan Boyle** for instance - are still making headlines. Then there's the tennis star **Andy Murray** as well as all those Scottish bands…it's a very long list!

TOP TEN ISLAND EXPERIENCES

Colin Mackenzie is a well-known Edinburgh businessman, but he loves nothing better than to spend his holidays island-hopping around the Scottish islands. It's been a life-long obsession, so he was the ideal person to ask for his top ten island experiences.

1. **View of Muckle Flugga from Hermaness Hill on the Shetland Isle of Unst**
   Well worth the walk. This really is the end of the UK.

2. **Landing on the beach by Barra**
   Actually, just watching the plane land is almost as good!

3. **Looking at the sea from the Butt of Lewis**
   You don't even have to leave the car if it's windy! (But you may see whales if you do.)

4.

4. **Seeing Eshaness when a westerly wind is blowing**
   Unforgettable Shetland seascapes.

5. **The walk from Rackwick Bay to the Old Man of Hoy, Orkney**
   There's just enough time to do this on a single day trip!

5.

6. **Walking to Oronsay from Colonsay, the Inner Hebrides**
   Take your wellies and watch the tide times!

7. **The Machrie Moor Standing Stones on Arran**
   Plenty of atmosphere here, out on the fields with the hills beyond…

8. **The boat trip across Loch Scavaig, Elgol, Skye**
   It's an incredible Cuillin view even from the shore.

9. **Finlaggan, Islay**
   Historic clan place - use your imagination as you cross the wooden walkway.

10. **Maeshowe, Orkney**
    Crawling through the entrance takes you back 5,000 years. Mind-blowing!

7.

TOP TEN WILDLIFE

Who better to ask for their top ten wildlife experiences in Scotland than a Scottish Ornithologists' Club Member and contributor to BTO Bird Atlas? Make sure you place Alan Smith's recommendations on your must-visit list!

1. **The Bass Rock gannets, North Berwick**
   Take a boat trip (and a telephoto lens) from North Berwick. The boat departs from the Scottish Seabird Centre - a 5-star attraction overlooking the Firth of Forth complete with Discovery Centre and cameras, allowing you to zoom in on seabirds and marine life!

1.

2. **Red kites in Perthshire**
   You get blasé about spotting them on your walks. That's a sign they're thriving! If you like what you see, you should also head to The Galloway Red Kite Trail in Dumfries & Galloway for another chance to view this beautiful species.

3. **Ospreys at Loch Garten, Abernethy**
   Or at several other places in Scotland. Spectacular - but in spring/summer only.

4. **Waders in the John Muir Country Park, Tyninghame, near Dunbar**
   When the tide goes out, it's like a scene from 'The Riddle of the Sands'.

5. **Overwintering grey geese, Loch of Strathbeg, Aberdeenshire**
   Scotland's largest land-locked lagoon.

6. **Alpine flowers on Meall nan Tarmachan, Perthshire**
   Less busy than its neighbour, Ben Lawers.

7. **Otters at Loch Druidibeg, Outer Hebrides**
   Just keep your eyes open and don't make too much noise.

8. **Seabird colonies, Marwick Head, Orkney**
   Scary cliffs, but a great spectacle.

9. **Bottle-nose dolphins in the Moray Firth, north east coast**
   You just never know where they'll pop up next. That's the fun part.

10. **Red squirrels on the bird tables, Landmark, Carrbridge**
    Very cheeky - but you can't begrudge them the peanuts.

TOP TEN MUSIC/ARTS VENUES

Hailing from the 'granite city' of Aberdeen, Michael Baigrie is a respected artist and teacher. Here he shares his top ten music and arts venues from across the country.

2.

1. **Dundee Rep Theatre, Dundee**
   Home to Scotland's only full-time resident company of actors and contemporary dancers.

2. **Oran Mor, Glasgow**
   Wide-ranging, vibrant - always a lot going on.

3. **Pitlochry Festival Theatre, Perthshire**
   A reminder that quality and active arts venues are often found outside the cities.

4. **National Galleries of Scotland**
   Their collection of Scottish and international art housed in five galleries across Scotland is amongst the best in the world, open daily and entry is free.

5. **The Lemon Tree, Aberdeen**
   Drama, comedy, music and more - all year round.

6. **Mull Theatre, Isle of Mull**
   One of Scotland's leading touring companies as well.

7. **Duff House, Banff**
   Sometimes overlooked but keep an eye on the classy events programme.

3.

8. **Hootananny, Inverness**
   Traditional Scottish pub offering a fine selection of malt whisky, local ales and live music every night.

9. **The Byre Theatre, St Andrews**
   Scotland's only 5-star arts attraction.

10. **The Fergusson Gallery, Perth**
    Celebrate the life and work of John Duncan Fergusson and his lifelong partner, Margaret Morris. Fergusson is best known as one of the Scottish Colourists and Morris one of the great pioneers of modern dance.

TOP TEN FOOD AND DRINK

Christopher Trotter from the Kingdom of Fife is a well-known Scottish chef with over 25 years of experience both in Scotland and internationally. He is passionate about locally sourced produce. Here are his top ten food and drink experiences…

1. **The Apron Stage, Stanley**
   Tiny restaurant close to Perth.
   Well worth discovering.

2. **Simon Macdonald's Smokehouse, Glenuig**
   Can't get much more away from it all on the Scottish mainland - and he makes the best smoked cheese.

3. **Dunvalanree in Carradale**
   This family run establishment provides meals cooked with care and passion.

4. **The Abbotsford, Edinburgh**
   Still a city 'institution' after all these years.

   5.

5. **Creel Restaurant, St Margaret's Hope, Orkney**
   Long established and still a firm favourite.

6. **The Wee Chippy, Anstruther**
   Anstruther is famous for its fish and chips.
   Pay a visit to the local's favourite - The Wee Chippy.

7. **Loch Bay Restaurant, Stein, Skye**
   Crab, lobster and much more - plus the perfect sunset.

8. **Loch Arthur Cheese, Dumfries**
   Fabulous cheese maker, Barry Graham.

   8.

9. **Royan, craft butchers, Elgin**
   One of Scotland's oldest butchers.
   Top grade, local, traceable meat, but affordable.

10. **The bar at Cottier's, Glasgow**
    Great in summer, outside drinking.
    Popular with trendy West Enders.

TOP TEN VISITORS' ATTRACTIONS

Johanna Campbell lives in the Scottish Borders and has enjoyed a long and successful career within the Scottish Tourism industry. Currently working as a top tour guide and planner, Johanna has an extensive knowledge of Scotland. For a great day out, the following attractions would be top of her list!

1. **Edinburgh Castle**
   Original and best - just because it's popular doesn't mean you shouldn't go!

2. **Kelvingrove Art Gallery and Museum, Glasgow**
   A great cultural focal point for the city of Glasgow.

3. **Museum of Scottish Lighthouses, Fraserburgh**
   Definitely different - the knowledgeable guides bring it alive.

4. **Traquair House, Scottish Borders**
   The real thing - a family home that has seen a lot of history. Brews beer too.

5. **Fyvie Castle, Aberdeenshire**
   Historic castle on a grand scale. Great art collection. Unsettling ghost is a bonus.

6. **Culloden, near Inverness**
   Informative, dispassionate, vivid portrayal of this famous battle.

7. **Burns National Heritage Park, Ayr**
   Teach yourself about Scotland's national poet. What does Tam o' Shanter mean anyway?

8. **Mount Stuart, Bute**
   Visually stunning Gothic stately home. Lose yourself in the vast gardens.

9. **Skara Brae, Orkney**
   If you had to live in the Stone Age, then this is where you'd choose to be. Cosy.

10. **Inverewe Garden, Wester Ross**
    It's temperate - not sub-tropical. But still a hugely popular tribute to the Gulf Stream.

3.

10.

● ●

TOP TEN GOLF COURSES

Scotland is renowned the world over as The Home of Golf, so it's no surprise that the quality of golf on offer is second to none! What's more, we have a long list of successful names within the sport. Callum Stephen hopes to follow in the footsteps of some of the greats. A club golfer and caddie at Gullane, here are his top ten courses!

1. **Castle Stuart Golf Links, near Inverness**
   Scotland's new generation of courses - this one is stunning.

2. **Askernish, South Uist**
   Fascinating - Old Tom Morris masterpiece
   of 1891, rediscovered and restored.

3. **Machrihanish Dunes, Argyll**
   The first new course to be built
   on the west coast for a century.

4. **Royal Dornoch, Sutherland**
   Classic coastal links still referred to as
   'The St Andrews of the North'.

   4.

5. **Cruden Bay, Aberdeenshire**
   Dunes and sea breezes - another old
   established links course.

6. **Musselburgh Links,**
   The Old Golf Course, East Lothian
   Officially the world's oldest golf course.

7. **Southernness, Dumfries & Galloway**
   Highly rated by those in the know.
   Breathtaking views and first class golf.

   5.

8. **Western Gailes, by Irvine, Ayrshire**
   The distillation of the huge choice of courses
   along the Clyde coast. Originally built for Glasgow merchants.

9. **Boat of Garten, Highlands**
   The genius of James Braid, laid out amongst
   the birchwoods. Accuracy imperative.

10. **New Course, St Andrews, Kingdom of Fife**
    Often regarded as the oldest 'new course' in the world.

ACCOMMODATION

When you pay to stay away, you want to discover that special something that makes you look forward to going back with much anticipation.

Perhaps it's the memory of relaxing with a book in an Edwardian drawing room, breakfasting in a Georgian kitchen, or enjoying tea in a Victorian conservatory. The unique surroundings - fine art, literature, period furniture, antiques. An exceptional room - a four-poster, an original fire place, an over-sized roll-top bath. A view like no other - over sea or loch, or across an ancient sun-kissed cityscape. The tranquil grounds - a walled garden, waterside walks, or a mysterious pond. Award-winning cuisine - fresh local produce, vintage wine and malt whisky collections.

From the ultimate in 5-star grand hotel accommodation to the secluded self-catering croft, from the boutique hotel to rustic B&B - you'll find all of these gems over the next few pages.

NETHER STRAVANNAN

Mount Stuart, Isle of Bute PA20 9LR
01700 503 877
contactus@mountstuart.com **Self-Catering**
www.mountstuart.com ★★★★

This luxurious self-catering development is situated on the attractive south west coast of the island. Its picturesque setting provides exceptional views over Arran, with Stravannan beach just 15 minutes' walk away. Up to 16 guests can enjoy the sanctuary of these beautifully furnished private lodges - ideally situated next to the Kingarth golf course and just a mile from the warm hospitality of the Kingarth Hotel and Smiddy Bar. Both North Lodge and South Lodge provide immaculate and spacious living space for family holidays, corporate weekends, wedding parties and relaxing breaks. A basket of fresh local produce awaits your arrival.

CLAN DONALD SKYE

Armadale, Sleat, Isle of Skye IV45 8RS
01471 844 305
office@clandonald.com
www.clandonald.com

Self-Catering
★★★★

Escape to the beauty and tranquillity of the Isle of Skye and visit Clan Donald Skye incorporating the romantic ruined Armadale Castle and Gardens, The Museum of the Isles, our family friendly 4-star self-catering lodges, nature trails and woodland walks, wedding and conference venue, library and study centre, plus restaurant and gift shop - all with glorious views across the Sound of Sleat. Open March to November - self-catering available all year.

DUISDALE COUNTRY HOUSE HOTEL & RESTAURANT

Isle Ornsay, Sleat, Isle of Skye IV43 8QW
01471 833 202
info@duisdale.com
www.duisdale.com

Country House Hotel
★★★★

Duisdale House Hotel is a small, wildly romantic hotel, located on the Isle of Skye with a range of sleek, contemporary rooms with sea or garden views and stylish four-poster bedrooms. Winner of Boutique Hotel of the Year 2009 the hotel restaurant offers two stylish zones; a handsome room with a real fire linked to a conservatory area with grand garden views. Luxurious garden hot-tub and memorable daily sailing trips on board a luxury yacht from April to September.

TORAVAIG HOUSE HOTEL & RESTAURANT

Sleat, Isle of Skye IV44 8RE
01471 820 200
info@skyehotel.co.uk
www.skyehotel.co.uk

Small Hotel
★★★★

Toravaig House Hotel and Restaurant is a romantic, boutique hotel with views to the Sound of Sleat. It has nine contemporary individually designed bedrooms and an award-winning restaurant. 2 AA rosettes. Highlands and Islands Restaurant of the Year 2009/2010 and winner of Highland Dining Out Experience 2009. Perfect for short breaks and intimate celebrations. Exclusive daily sailing trips on board a luxury yacht from April to September.

BRAIGHE HOUSE

20 Braighe Road, Stornoway,
Isle of Lewis HS2 0BQ
01851 705 287

Guest House alison@braighehouse.co.uk
★★★★★ **Gold** www.braighehouse.co.uk

Braighe House offers 5-star Gold accommodation on a
stunning sea-front location on the edge of Stornoway.
Guests will enjoy an exceptional breakfast using fresh
local produce from a comprehensive and diverse menu.
Golfing, cycling and fishing equipment can also be hired
directly from Braighe House to ensure you make the most of the local area. Car hire is
also available with free pick up service at either airport or ferry terminal in Stornoway.

HEBRIDEAN LUXURY HOLIDAYS

29 Kenneth Street, Stornoway,
Isle of Lewis HS1 2DR **Self-Catering**
0800 234 3271 ★★★★★
info@hebrideanluxuryholidays.co.uk
www.hebrideanluxuryholidays.co.uk

Luxurious 5-star self-catering timber lodges built
using environmentally sensitive methods and
materials, offering everything you need for a break on Lewis.
Morag is on hand to help you get the most from your holiday, with advice on car hire,
food hampers and where to eat and shop. Nothing is too much trouble.

BROAD BAY HOUSE

Back, Nr Stornoway, Isle of Lewis HS2 0LQ
01851 820 990

Guest House stay@broadbayhouse.co.uk
★★★★★ **Gold** www.broadbayhouse.co.uk

Broad Bay House is set in an outstanding beachside
location just 15 minutes from Stornoway. Purpose
designed and built as a luxury guest house, it delivers
a fantastic combination of fine contemporary
accommodation and great local food. Four luxury
en-suite guest bedrooms and a spectacular lounge/
dining room overlooking the bay, completing
this exclusive top quality retreat. VisitScotland 5-star Gold and
EatScotland Silver rated.

HOTEL HEBRIDES

Pier Road, Tarbert, Isle of Harris HS3 3DG
01859 502 364
stay@hotel-hebrides.com
www.hotel-hebrides.com

Hotel
★★★★

Hotel Hebrides is a boutique-style hotel offering
quality accommodation and award-winning food
on the Hebridean Isle of Harris off the west coast of
Scotland. The spectacular scenery, unspoilt white
sandy beaches and turquoise waters are the perfect
backdrop for the sublime comfort and exceptional food you'll find here. The 23 individually
designed en-suite bedrooms are chic and stylish with designer statement beds and bold
colour schemes, crisp white linen, luxurious bath oils, state-of-the-art TVs and Wi-Fi.

BLUE REEF COTTAGES

5 Scaristavore, Isle of Harris HS3 3HX
01859 550 370
info@stay-hebrides.com
www.stay-hebrides.com

Self-Catering
★★★★★

Offering 5-star luxury in a world-class location. From the
comfort of your cottage enjoy the spectacular views,
local beaches and panoramic scenery of the Atlantic
Ocean and nearby hills. The cottages are unique in their
design with turf roof and stone walls. Each cottage is
totally private and is fully equipped with sauna, jacuzzi
bath and wood/peat burning stove. For the ultimate 5-star experience Blue Reef
Cottages is the perfect Hebridean retreat. The cottages have also been given a Gold
award from the Green Tourism Business Scheme.

THE SMIDDY

Burnside Croft, 2 Borve,
Isle of Berneray, North Uist HS6 5BJ
01876 540 235
burnsidecroft@hebrides.net
www.burnsidecroft.com

Self-Catering
★★★★★

The former Smiddy at Burnside Croft has been renovated
to an extremely high standard, incorporating energy
saving technology. It will provide a relaxing hideaway
for one or two people, with stunning views across the
machair and sunsets beyond the dunes. The accommodation comprises an open-plan living
area. The bedroom area has either a large double or twin beds as required, with an en-suite
whirlpool bath. Suitable for assisted wheelchair access.

HOLLAND HOUSE

Harray, Orkney KW17 2LQ
01856 771 400
info@hollandhouseorkney.co.uk
www.hollandhouseorkney.co.uk

Bed & Breakfast
★★★★★

Holland House offers 5-star luxury accommodation in
a beautifully appointed former country manse situated
near Orkney's famous World Heritage Sites and excellent
free trout fishing lochs. Birdwatching and walking are
also popular attractions for visitors. In addition to the
well appointed bedrooms, all with en-suite facilities,
there is a spacious residents' lounge with an open fire
and a conservatory leading into a large walled garden with private parking.

RICKLA

Harray, Orkney KW17 2JT
01856 761 575
stewart@rickla.com
www.rickla.com

Self-Catering
★★★★★

Secluded, wonderfully quiet, supremely luxurious self-
catering for two to four on the edge of Orkney's World
Heritage Site. Centrally situated, on a private track, well
away from traffic yet only a 10 minute drive to Kirkwall
or Stromness. Bedroom suites have private sun lounges
with spectacular views of the neolithic heartland of Orkney.
Thistle award-winning owners and rated in VisitScotland's top
four self-catering properties.

THE LYNNFIELD HOTEL AND RESTAURANT

Holm Road, St Ola, Kirkwall,
Orkney KW15 1SU
01856 872 505
office@lynnfield.co.uk
www.lynnfieldhotel.com

Small Hotel
★★★★

People remark that from the outside, The Lynnfield
appears to be a modern building (c.1800). The inside
is anything but: very traditional and full of antiques,
especially its tranquil panelled lounge. The delicious cuisine is based around Orkney's
quality produce from steaks and scallops to Arctic charr and the unique North
Ronaldsay mutton.

INGASETTER

Glover Lodges, Cunningsburgh,
Shetland ZE2 9HA
01950 477 596

Self-Catering
★★★★★

info@gloverlodges.co.uk
www.gloverlodges.co.uk

Shetland - Britain's 'best kept secret' - with striking landscapes, rich wildlife and fascinating culture and heritage. Stay in 5-star luxury in the newly built 'Ingasetter' lodge finished to an exceptional standard and set in a unique and stunning location with magnificent uninterrupted sea-views. The perfect place for the discerning visitor who recognises the importance of beautiful surroundings, quality and comfort - where better to capture the true essence of Shetland's natural beauty?

LOCH NESS LODGE

Brachla, Loch Ness-side, Inverness IV3 8LA
01456 459 469
escape@loch-ness-lodge.com
www.loch-ness-lodge.com

**Restaurant
with Rooms**
★★★★★ **Gold**

With seven luxurious, individually styled bedrooms, elegant drawing rooms and a Spa and Therapy suite, Loch Ness Lodge offers its guests an experience of absolute refinement and relaxation. Award-winning fine dining; discrete service with a personal touch; and sumptuous surroundings in a beautiful setting overlooking the mysterious Loch Ness, all combine to make a stay at Loch Ness Lodge unforgettable.

POOL HOUSE HOTEL

Highland, Poolewe, Ross-shire IV22 2LD
01445 781 272

**Guest
Accommodation**
★★★★★ **Gold**

enquiries@pool-house.co.uk
www.pool-house.co.uk

This former fishing lodge and one-time WWII headquarters is today decorated throughout with eccentric opulence. Treasures include a copy of Napoleon's bed, authentic Titanic memorabilia, Chinese statues, gold-leaf screens, a maharaja's four-poster, gothic furniture from a church and decorative Greek pots. Expect hand-painted walls, a full-size billiard table and quaint Victorian canopied or marble baths. Good food is accompanied by fine wines. A whole room is dedicated to malt whisky.

BLYTHSWOOD SQUARE

Hotel
Awaiting Grading

11 Blythswood Square,
Glasgow G2 4AD
0141 248 8888
reserve@blythswoodsquare.com
www.blythswoodsquare.com

Blythswood Square, in Glasgow city centre, houses 100 guest rooms including a penthouse. Not to mention a restaurant, the perfect place to enjoy delicious, seasonal, local food and inventive cocktails, and The Rally Bar, named after the Monte Carlo Rally, which started out from Blythswood Square in 1955. There is also a 35 metre Salon with stunning views over Blythswood Square and there will also be Glasgow's first luxury spa.

23 MAYFIELD

23 Mayfield Gardens,
Edinburgh EH9 2BX
0131 667 5806
info@23mayfield.co.uk
www.23mayfield.co.uk

Guest House
★★★★ Gold

23 Mayfield is a family run Victorian detached guest house built in 1868. Situated 1 mile from Edinburgh's Royal Mile the guest house offers easy access to Edinburgh Castle, Holyrood Palace and Princes Street. To enable you to have a comfortable stay it has a residents' drawing room (refreshments available), free off-street parking, award-winning breakfast, Wi-Fi and bike hire. Four-poster rooms available. On main bus route. Local bars and restaurants.

CHANNINGS

Hotel
★★★★

12-16 South Learmonth Gardens,
Edinburgh EH4 1EZ
0131 315 2226
reserve@channings.co.uk
www.channings.co.uk

An informal, relaxed hotel with a very friendly approach, Channings occupies five Edwardian townhouses in Stockbridge. A wonderfully quirky property which feels a bit like a Scottish country home, full of charming Victorian paintings, prints, books, furniture and memorabilia. There are 41 bedrooms in all and one of the Channings townhouses was home to Sir Ernest Shackleton, the Antarctic explorer between 1904 and 1910.

PRESTONFIELD HOUSE

Priestfield Road, Edinburgh EH16 5UT

0131 225 7800

reservations@prestonfield.com **Hotel**

www.prestonfield.com ★★★★★ **Gold**

Historic charm, boutique chic and an unashamed sense of luxury and fun are the hallmarks of James Thomson's stylish reworking of Prestonfield. Opulence, theatre and luxury are combined in this former Lord Provost's mansion where minimalism is banished and maximalism rules! Alongside dramatic bedrooms and sumptuous suites, there is his destination restaurant - Rhubarb, and opulent salons, historic public rooms and ravishing gardens. Prestonfield - truly an A-list celebrity bolt-hole.

THE BONHAM

35 Drumsheugh Gardens,
Edinburgh EH3 7RN

0131 226 6050

Hotel reserve@thebonham.com
★★★★ www.thebonham.com

A boutique hotel with a very contemporary spirit, The Bonham occupies a series of Victorian buildings in the West End of Edinburgh, whose soaring natural proportions have created a truly dynamic set of rooms and public spaces. There are 48 boutique rooms and suites each individually styled, and Restaurant at the Bonham is a destination in its own right, renowned well beyond Scotland.

THE EDINBURGH RESIDENCE

7 Rothesay Terrace,
Edinburgh EH3 7RY **Town House Hotel**

0131 226 3380 ★★★★★

reserve@theedinburghresidence.com

www.theedinburghresidence.co.uk

The Edinburgh Residence, a 5-star hotel, is a collection of 29 elegant suites through three adjoining Victorian houses in the West End. The 5-star suites are more like apartments, with magnificent proportions that allow you to spread out and feel at home. Feeling more like a club than a hotel, it offers 24-hour room service and all the housekeeping, concierge and reception services you would associate with a 5-star hotel.

THE HOWARD

34 Great King Street,
Edinburgh EH3 6QH
0131 557 3500
reserve@thehoward.com
www.thehoward.com

**Town House
Hotel**
★★★★★

The Howard is an intimate and discreet luxury 5-star
hotel which occupies three Georgian townhouses in a
super-convenient location in the heart of Edinburgh's
New Town. Classically elegant both outside and in,
The Howard has just 18 luxury rooms and suites. A key
feature of The Howard is the collection of butlers, who take care of everything for you. The
Howard also has its own intimate restaurant, The Atholl.

THE WITCHERY
BY THE CASTLE

Castlehill, The Royal Mile,
Edinburgh EH1 2NF
0131 225 5613
mail@thewitchery.com
www.thewitchery.com

**Restaurant
with Rooms**
★★★★★ **Gold**

The Witchery's renowned suites are hidden in charming
historic buildings at Edinburgh Castle's gates. These
magical suites are the perfect antidote to bland, uniform hotels
and make an indulgent hide-away in the heart of Edinburgh's historic Old Town. Each
of the Witchery's uniquely-indulgent suites is filled with the personal touches that are
the hallmark of their creator, James Thomson - enjoy ultra-romantic gothic décor, quirky
antiques and roll-top baths for two.

CAIRNESS HOUSE

Lonmay, Fraserburgh,
Aberdeenshire AB43 8XP
01346 582 078
info@cairnesshouse.com
www.cairnesshouse.com

Bed & Breakfast
★★★★★

If you're looking for a mix of luxury and historic
surroundings, head for a stay at spectacular Cairness
House near the beautiful Buchan coast. Cairness is the
finest Greek Revival country house in Scotland and
offers 5-star accommodation for travellers seeking a rarefied and relaxing retreat. Sumptuous
four-poster beds, roll-top baths and sizzling breakfasts in the vast Georgian kitchen will
transport you to a bygone era.

MELDRUM HOUSE

Country House Hotel
★★★★

Oldmeldrum, Inverurie,
Aberdeenshire AB51 0AE
01651 872 294
enquiries@meldrumhouse.com
www.meldrumhouse.com

Set amidst beautiful countryside, The Meldrum House Country Hotel & Golf Course offers unrivalled quality. Only a few miles from Aberdeen, this is one of the finest luxury hotels Scotland has to offer. For a weekend break, wedding reception, conference or luxury golf vacation, you can enjoy great Scottish hospitality, fine dining and the tranquillity of the magnificent Meldrum Estate. If golf is your passion, it offers a range of golf vacation packages and golf breaks at the spectacular and challenging course.

THE MARCLIFFE HOTEL AND SPA

North Deeside Road,
Aberdeen AB15 9YA
01224 861 000
enquiries@marcliffe.com
www.marcliffe.com

Hotel
★★★★★

The Marcliffe Hotel and Spa is situated in 11-acres of wooded grounds on the outskirts of Aberdeen and is ideally located for visiting Scotland's scenic north east. The Conservatory Restaurant offers only seasonal Scottish produce, accompanied by a wine list of over 400 wines and more than 100 malt whiskies. In the design and preparation of the menus the chefs call on locally-grown vegetables to complement Scotland's finest fish, meat and game.

ARDEONAIG HOTEL

Small Hotel
★★★★

South Road, Loch Tay, Ardeonaig,
Perthshire FK21 8SU
01567 820 400
info@ardeonaighotel.co.uk
www.ardeonaighotel.co.uk

Ardeonaig Hotel, situated on the banks of Loch Tay, in rural Perthshire is a very special place, where guests can be assured of a memorable Highland experience. The award-winning cuisine reflects the changing seasons, and showcases the finest local produce available. Gourmet lovers will adore Ardeonaig's programme of food and wine events taking place throughout the year, from sumptuous tasting to presentations from guest chefs and winemakers happy to share their advice and tips.

THE GLENEAGLES HOTEL

Auchterarder, Perthshire PH3 1NF
0800 389 3737

Hotel
★★★★★ **Gold**

resort.sales@gleneagles.com
www.gleneagles.com

When the Gleneagles Hotel opened in 1924 it was described as 'a Riviera in the Highlands' and 'the 8th wonder of the world'. A member of Leading Hotels of the World, Gleneagles is set in 850-acres of Perthshire countryside, only an hour's drive from Edinburgh and Glasgow. Home to three top championship golf courses and a wide range of outdoor leisure activities, as well as an award-winning spa and a 2 Michelin star restaurant.

BAYVIEW

Drumeldrie, Upper Largo, Fife KY8 6JD
01333 360 454
margaret@bayviewfife.com   **Bed & Breakfast**
www.bayviewfife.com   ★★★★

You are assured a warm Scottish welcome at this delightful 19th century cottage. Situated in an idyllic location just 10 miles from St Andrews on a lane leading to the beach and Fife coastal path, Luxury en-suite accommodation, superb sea-views, sumptuous breakfasts featuring fresh local produce a speciality. Tailored golf breaks arranged. Personal service and attention to detail ensure a relaxing stay. For the evenings, EatScotland and Michelin award-winning restaurants nearby.

EASTER KINCAPLE

St Andrews, Fife KY16 9SG
01334 473 224

Bed & Breakfast
Awaiting
Grading

info@easterkincaple.com
www.easterkincaple.com

Easter Kincaple has been in the Cuthill family for 120 years. This elegant country home is 1.5 miles from the centre of St Andrews. Guests have the privacy and comfort of their own public rooms. The house, walled garden and working farmland is nestled in its own 750-acres. The estate borders with St Andrews, the seawall, golf courses and neighbouring villages. The views are breathtaking across the water, fields of seasonal crops and of course the all-familiar distinctive skyline of St Andrews.

RUFFLETS COUNTRY HOUSE

Strathkinness Low Road,
St Andrews, Fife KY16 9TX
01334 472 594
reservations@rufflets.co.uk
www.rufflets.co.uk

Country House Hotel
★★★★ Gold

Rufflets is one of the finest examples of a traditional country house hotel in Scotland, offering a range of individually styled bedrooms, an award-winning restaurant, and wonderful grounds and gardens. The warm comfortable public areas of the hotel offer a relaxed and intimate environment, all backed up with some of the best service around. A perfect base for exploring the delights of the Kingdom of Fife.

ALT NA CRAIG HOUSE

Glenmore Road, Oban, Argyll PA34 4PG
01631 564 524
contact@altnacraighouse.com
www.guesthouseinoban.com

Guest House
★★★★

Welcome to Alt na Craig House in Oban, where traditional Highland hospitality meets chic boutique comfort to offer you something that is 'just that little bit special'. This turreted Victorian house has been sympathetically refurbished to offer bed and breakfast in luxury boutique style accommodation, great service and attention to detail. Set in its own grounds with fantastic views over the bay, it is only a short walk into the town centre.

ARDS HOUSE

Connel, By Oban, Argyll PA37 1PT
01631 710 255
info@ardshouse.com
www.ardshouse.com

Guest House
★★★★ Gold

Only 5 minutes from Oban, in a truly idyllic location with breathtaking views and incredible sunsets. Ards House combines modern facilities and comforts with the traditional ambience of a Victorian villa. An excellent base to explore the west Highlands or simply relax and unwind. Only a personal visit can do justice to any description of the splendid views from the windows out over the waters of the Firth of Lorn and the sunsets over the Morven hills beyond. Exclusive to non-smokers.

ARDANAISEIG HOTEL

Kilchrenan by Taynuilt, Argyll PA35 1HE

01866 833 333

info@ardanaiseig.com

www.ardanaiseig.com

Country House Hotel
★★★★

At the foot of Ben Cruachan, hidden in 240-acres of deeply wooded gardens on the banks of Loch Awe, lies Ardanaiseig - a truly magical Highland getaway. The 4-star, baronial-style country house offers 14 bedrooms, a self-catering cottage and a private Boatshed Suite, all offering spectacular views and each individually designed to offer a choice of traditional or contemporary accommodation. Known as a food lovers' hotel, guests never fail to delight in Chef de Cuisine, Gary Goldie's, 7-course tasting menus, incorporating the finest local and international ingredients.

CROMLIX HOUSE HOTEL

Country House Hotel
★★★★

Kinbuck, Dunblane, Stirlingshire FK15 9JT

01786 822 125

reservations@cromlixhouse.com

www.cromlixhouse.com

Cromlix House is set in a beautiful 2,000-acre estate near Stirling. It is only a 35 minute drive from Glasgow and a 50 minute drive from Edinburgh. It is easily accessible by car, rail and air. The House is furnished throughout with antiques, fine furnishing and paintings. In the winter all the public rooms are lit with roaring log fires. It is easy to feel relaxed here and the grounds are an oasis of tranquillity and seclusion. Cromlix is a world apart.

TURNBERRY RESORT

Maidens Road, Turnberry, Ayrshire KA26 9LT

01655 331 000

turnberry@luxurycollection.com

www.turnberryresort.co.uk

Hotel
★★★★★

Nestled on the rugged west coast of Scotland you will find the iconic Turnberry Resort, Scotland. A 5-star destination where you can enjoy sophisticated accommodation, world-class golf, revitalising spa treatments, thrilling outdoor pursuits and exquisite dining or afternoon tea experiences. The newly renovated guest accommodations have been delightfully designed to keep the discerning visitor to Scotland beautifully cocooned.

GLENAPP CASTLE

Ballantrae, Girvan, Ayrshire KA26 0NZ
01465 831 212

Hotel   info@glenappcastle.com
★★★★★ **Gold**   www.glenappcastle.com

This Scottish Baronial Castle is set amidst 30-acres of
magnificent gardens and woodland on the beautiful
Ayrshire coast, just 90 minutes south of Glasgow.
The castle offers internationally renowned standards
of quality and service, as well as superb fine dining
in its 3 AA Rosette-winning restaurant, the perfect
setting to enjoy a mouth-watering taste of the finest
Scottish produce.

THE WHEATSHEAF AT SWINTON

Main Street, Swinton,   **Restaurant**
Berwickshire TD11 3JJ   **with Rooms**
01890 860 257   ★★★★
reception@wheatsheaf-swinton.co.uk
www.wheatsheaf-swinton.co.uk

Family run, award-winning Restaurant with Rooms.
First class food with the freshest of local ingredients
including daily fish deliveries from Eyemouth. Excellent wine list including selection of 12
by the glass and 50 Scottish Single Malts. Cosy, comfortable country accommodation with
friendly and attentive service; the ideal base to discover the beautiful Scottish Borders.
View all facilities on the virtual tour section of the website.

WHITEHOUSE

St Boswells, Roxburghshire
Bed & Breakfast   TD6 0ED
★★★★★   01573 460 343
staying@whitehousecountryhouse.com
www.whitehousecountryhouse.com

Luxury accommodation in an outstanding
location in the central borders with south-facing
views of the Tweed Valley and Cheviot hills.
Spacious bedrooms and bathrooms - with large
fluffy towels and bathrobes. Open log fires.
Delicious home cooked yet stylish dinners - and an extensive breakfast
menu. Perfect for a relaxing break or for meeting up with friends for a celebration.

EATING OUT

What makes Scotland's eateries so special? Could it be the fresh local produce - the abundance of seafood, the internationally acclaimed beef and lamb, the vast array of cheeses and native berries? Or is it the landscape in which they lie? After all, you can savour hand-dived scallops while you watch a wild otter cavort in the very same sea-loch beyond the window. Inspiring - certainly, but we'd venture there's something more: and that's the real people who run these establishments. Scotland's dedicated chefs are always on hand - so it's no wonder the experience is so special. For a whole host of restaurant choices, *EatScotland.com* is the ideal website to visit. Read on to discover a list of extra special Gold EatScotland award-winning restaurants.

KINLOCH LODGE

Sleat, Isle of Skye IV43 8QY
01471 833 333 www.kinloch-lodge.co.uk

Escape from the city and unwind at the exquisite Kinloch Lodge. This fine home under the direction of Lord and Lady Macdonald and their family provides excellent quality food using fresh local produce whenever possible, within comfortable and relaxed period surroundings. The menu has a varied theme and caters for most dietary requirements. All the produce is sourced locally.

THE THREE CHIMNEYS RESTAURANT

Colbost, Dunvegan, Isle of Skye IV55 8ZT
01470 511 258 www.threechimneys.co.uk

It is rare that the food in any restaurant truly reflects its location quite as much as it does at The Three Chimneys on the Isle of Skye, something that has contributed to the restaurant's huge popularity over two decades, along with the skilled expertise of acclaimed head chef, Michael Smith. Restaurant critic for The New York Times, Frank Bruni, has also announced that this restaurant is one of his personal top five favourite restaurants in the world.

INVERLOCHY CASTLE HOTEL

Torlundy, Fort William PH33 6SN
01397 702 177   www.inverlochycastlehotel.com

The menu features modern British cuisine which is internationally recognised by all major guides. Awarded 3 AA Rosettes and 1 Michelin Star, the cuisine is seriously devoted to fresh ingredients of the highest quality, many from the Castle's own gardens or smokehouse.

LOCH NESS LODGE

Brachla, Loch Ness-side, Inverness IV3 8LA
01456 459 469   www.loch-ness-lodge.com

Loch Ness Lodge is an elegant and intimate retreat in the heart of the Scottish Highlands overlooking the mysterious and beautiful Loch Ness. Using the finest, fresh, local ingredients, the kitchen produces dish after dish of complex variety and delicious invention.

21212

3 Royal Terrace, Edinburgh EH7 5AB
0131 523 1030   www.21212restaurant.co.uk

21212 is a luxury fine dining restaurant with Michelin-starred chef Paul Kitching at the helm of the adventurous menu which offers a unique 5-course gourmet menu. Situated in Edinburgh's New Town in a Grade A listed building, 21212 offers a private dining room as well as four super bedrooms in a wonderful tranquil location which is, unbelievably, less than 10 minutes walk from Waverley Station.

RESTAURANT MARTIN WISHART

54 The Shore, Edinburgh EH6 6RA
0131 553 3557   www.martin-wishart.co.uk

Situated on the shore overlooking the Water of Leith, the eponymous restaurant combines a calm and welcoming ambience with superb modern French cuisine, using the freshest ingredients sourced from throughout Scotland. The menu changes regularly to incorporate the best of seasonal produce. Wines are carefully selected to suit the menus and the list is continually updated.

THE KITCHIN

78 Commercial Quay, Leith, Edinburgh EH6 6LX
0131 555 1755 www.thekitchin.com

Dining at The Kitchin is relaxed and welcoming where the food is the focus. The passion of Tom and Michaela and their entire team shines through in what they deliver; quality and consistency. The restaurant showcases chef Tom Kitchin's unique marriage of seasonal Scottish produce with the classical French techniques he has mastered working alongside some of the world's greatest chefs.

63 TAY STREET

63 Tay Street, Perth PH2 8NN
01738 441 451 www.63taystreet.com

Smart, contemporary in style, cosy and welcoming, 63 Tay Street commands excellent views across the Tay in the heart of Perth. If you delight in unusual ingredients, innovative cooking, robust, authentic flavours and the sheer pleasure of sitting down to enjoy superb craftsmanship, this is the place for you.

RESTAURANT ANDREW FAIRLIE

The Gleneagles Hotel, Auchterarder PH3 1NF
01764 694 267 www.andrewfairlie.co.uk

Andrew Fairlie creates signature dishes in his intimate, 2 Michelin-starred restaurant, where every detail has been carefully planned to create a truly special experience. Many of the ingredients for Andrew's gourmet menu come from the famous Rungis market outside Paris as well as from local Scottish suppliers. Try Andrew's signature dish 'Smoked Lobster' which involves smoking lobster shells over old whisky barrels for up to 12 hours.

MONACHYLE MHOR HOTEL

Balquhidder, Lochearnhead, Perthshire FK19 8PQ
01877 384 622 www.mhor.net

The restaurant prides itself on using the best of what it can gather within a 30-mile radius. The restaurant has a daily-changing dinner menu, all the fish being sourced direct from the boat and delivered overnight, including hand-dived scallops from Shetland and Orkney, and fresh oysters from Tongue. The style of the food is modern Scottish, but always striving to evolve and offer good value for money.

THE GREEN INN RESTAURANT

9 Victoria Road, Ballater, Aberdeenshire AB35 5QQ
01339 755 701 www.green-inn.com

The Green Inn is an unobtrusive, vernacular stone building fronting on to the attractive 'village green' in the centre of Ballater. What lies behind the modest frontage is an unexpectedly spacious temple to good food. Only the best and freshest produce is used, wherever possible sourced locally, to produce mouth-watering dishes with great care and skill.

THE AIRDS HOTEL AND RESTAURANT

Port Appin, Argyll PA38 4DF
01631 730 236 www.airds-hotel.com

Dinner is an occasion at The Airds Hotel, providing a romantic atmosphere suited to socialising with friends or loved ones. The lounges enable you to wind down and relax before and after dinner, while the highly trained staff ensure your meal is served with a balance between formality and friendliness. The overall ambiance of this venue is quality with a level of attention to detail which is rarely found.

GLENAPP CASTLE RESTAURANT

Glenapp Castle, Ballantrae, Girvan,
Ayrshire KA26 0NZ
01465 831 212 www.glenappcastle.com

This Scottish Baronial Castle is set amidst 30-acres of magnificent gardens and woodland on the beautiful Ayrshire coast, just 90 minutes south of Glasgow. The castle offers internationally renowned standards and service, as well as superb fine dining in its 3 AA Rosette and EatScotland Gold award-winning restaurant, the perfect setting to enjoy a mouth-watering taste of the finest Scottish produce.

THE HORSESHOE INN

Eddleston, by Peebles EH45 8QP
01721 730 225 www.horseshoeinn.co.uk

Originally a Blacksmith's shop, The Horseshoe Inn is situated in the sleepy village of Eddleston in the Scottish Borders, 5 miles north of Peebles and only 18 miles south of Edinburgh. The deep sofas in the lounge allow guests to enjoy drinks before dinner, and an eye-catching, smart bistro provides an appealing alternative to the more formal Bardoulet's Restaurant.

HOW TO GET THERE

It's never been easier to join us in Scotland. With so many low-cost, hassle-free options to choose from, you will be here in no time!

By Air: Scotland is well served by a range of carriers, from *British Airways* to a number of budget airlines, all operating from airports around London and from other regional hubs.

Flying is the quickest and easiest way to travel if you're heading out to the Highlands and Islands and with competitive airfares on popular routes from London, you are sure to find a package to suit your needs. For *British Airways* operated flights, reservations and general enquiries please call **0844 493 0787** or visit **www.britishairways.com**

By Rail: There are direct daily services to Scotland from almost every major train station in England. From Kent to the Kingdom of Fife or London to Loch Lomond, there are a number of train operators to choose from. Simply contact *National Rail Enquiries* to find out more: **0845 748 4950** or **www.nationalrail.co.uk**

By Car: Set off for Scotland behind the wheel, and travel in the comfort of your own car. You can use the *M1*, moving on to the *M6* before entering the *A74* into Scotland. Alternatively, why not take the *A7* via Carlisle where you can explore winding country roads and stunning scenery as you enter the Scottish Borders. Or if you want to admire the east coast, make your way for the *A1* and admire the views.

GETTING AROUND

By Road: Scotland has a great road network covering most parts of the country, with motorways and dual carriageway roads linking most cities and major towns. You can even drive all the way to one of Scotland's largest islands - the Isle of Skye - via the Skye Road Bridge which is accessible from the Kyle of Lochalsh on the mainland.

By Ferry: There are sixty inhabited islands within Scotland, and nearly fifty of them have scheduled ferry links. Most ferries carry cars and vans, and the vast majority can be booked in advance.

If you want to travel to the Islands of the Clyde or the Outer Hebrides, your main choice will be *Caledonian MacBrayne* (generally abbreviated to *CalMac*). They sail to over twenty one islands altogether, and they offer reduced-fare passes which offer great savings on multiple crossings.

For further information contact: *CalMac* - **0800 066 5000** or **www.calmac.co.uk**

For ferry crossings to the Orkney and Shetland Islands, *Northlink Ferries* operate nightly crossings from Aberdeen whilst Scrabster near Thurso operates several daily crossings to Stromness in Orkney. Contact - **0845 6000 449** or **www.northlinkferries.co.uk**

Alternatively, *Pentland Ferries* run a car ferry from Gills Bay near John o'Groats to St Margaret's Hope in Orkney, while *John o'Groats Ferries* operate a summer-only passenger ferry from John o'Groats to Burwick in Orkney.

Pentland Ferries - **01856 831 226** or **www.pentlandferries.co.uk**
John o'Groats Ferries - **01955 611 353** or **www.jogferry.co.uk**

The various Orkney Isles are linked to each other by services run by *Orkney Ferries*, and *Shetland Inter-island Ferries* operate a similar service to link the Isles.

Orkney Ferries - **01856 872 044** or **www.orkneyferries.co.uk**
Shetland Inter-island Ferries - **01595 693 535** or **www.shetland.gov.uk/ferries**

By Plane: Apart from its five main airports of Glasgow, Glasgow Prestwick, Edinburgh, Aberdeen and Inverness, Scotland has a number of smaller airports, many of them on the islands, some of which are little more than gravel airstrips while one - on the island of Barra - has its landing strip on a beach! There are a wide range of interconnecting flights between each of these and the main hubs.

Most flights are operated by *Flybe*. For inter-island flights in Shetland (excluding Fair Isle), you need to book direct through *Loganair*. Other services between the mainland and Stornoway are provided by *Eastern Airways*. Also, *Loch Lomond Seaplanes* operate flights from Glasgow to Oban, and Tobermory on Mull.

Flybe - **0871 700 2000** or **www.flybe.com**
Loganair - **0871 700 2000** or **www.loganair.co.uk**
Eastern Airways - **08703 669 100** or **www.easternairways.com**
Loch Lomond Seaplanes - **01436 675 030** or **www.lochlomondseaplanes.com**